AWESOME *Sauce*

*Create Videos to Inspire Students,
Engage Parents and Save You Time*

JOSH STOCK

International Society for Technology in Education
PORTLAND, OR • ARLINGTON, VA

AWESOME SAUCE
Create Videos to Inspire Students, Engage Parents and Save You Time
Josh Stock

Director of Books and Journals: Colin Murcray
Acquisitions Editor: Valerie Witte
Production Editor: Stephanie Argy
Copy Editor: Ernesto Yermoli
Proofreader: Joanna Szabo
Indexer: Kento Ikeda
Book Design and Production: Danielle Foster
Cover Design: Edwin Ouellette
Peer Reviewers: Gregory Gilmore, Shaundel Krumheuer, Krishna R. Millsapp, Allison Thompson
ISTE Standards Reviewers: Nicole Cooper, Baila Spielman, Angie Sutherland, Holly Veith

Library of Congress Cataloging-in-Publication Data

Names: Stock, Joshua, author.

Title: Awesome sauce : create videos to inspire students, engage parents and save you time / Joshua Stock.

Description: First edition. | Portland, OR : International Society for Technology in Education, [2020] | Includes bibliographical references and index. | Summary: "The ability to use video to communicate has become a basic element of literacy - inside and outside the classroom. This playful, fun-to-read book by award-winning educator Josh Stock shows educators how to make simple videos that explain assignments, welcome students to new schools and grades, differentiate lessons for a range of learning levels and more. The book also helps teachers use video to address common issues like enhancing classroom culture and managing parent communication. Structured like a cookbook, Awesome Sauce discusses both the "why" and the "how" behind the strategies. Each section begins with the story of why Stock uses the strategy, demonstrating what teachers will get out of trying it with their students. These explanations are followed by "how-to" recipes that guide readers in creating the "awesome sauce" their videos will become"-- Provided by publisher.

Identifiers: LCCN 2020004996 (print) | LCCN 2020004997 (ebook) | ISBN 9781564848499 (paperback) | ISBN 9781564848475 (epub) | ISBN 9781564848468 (mobi) | ISBN 9781564848482 (pdf)

Subjects: LCSH: Video tapes in education | Teaching--Methodology. | Effective teaching. | Teacher-student relationships.

Classification: LCC LB1044.75 .S76 2020 (print) | LCC LB1044.75 (ebook) | DDC 371.33/5--dc23

LC record available at https://lccn.loc.gov/2020004996

LC ebook record available at https://lccn.loc.gov/2020004997

First Edition

ISBN: 978-1-56484-849-9

Ebook version available

Printed in the United States of America

ISTE® is a registered trademark of the International Society for Technology in Education.

ABOUT ISTE

The International Society for Technology in Education (ISTE) is a nonprofit organization that works with the global education community to accelerate the use of technology to solve tough problems and inspire innovation. Our worldwide network believes in the potential technology holds to transform teaching and learning.

ISTE sets a bold vision for education transformation through the ISTE Standards, a framework for students, educators, administrators, coaches and computer science educators to rethink education and create innovative learning environments. ISTE hosts the annual ISTE Conference & Expo, one of the world's most influential edtech events. The organization's professional learning offerings include online courses, professional networks, year-round academies, peer-reviewed journals and other publications. ISTE is also the leading publisher of books focused on technology in education. For more information or to become an ISTE member, visit iste.org. Subscribe to ISTE's YouTube channel and connect with ISTE on Twitter, Facebook and LinkedIn.

Related ISTE Titles

STEAM Power: Infusing Art Into Your STEM Curriculum, by Tim Needles (2020)

Power Up Your Classroom: Reimagine Learning Through Gameplay, by Lindsey Blass and Cate Tolnai (2019)

Sketchnoting in the Classroom: A Practical Guide to Deepen Student Learning, by Nichole Carter (2019)

To see all books available from ISTE, please visit id.iste.org/resources.

ABOUT THE AUTHOR

Josh Stock is a sixth-grade language arts teacher at Santa Fe Trail Middle School in Olathe, Kansas, and an Awesomeness Expert. He has served on the Building Leadership Team through the Mercury phase of the school's Kansans Can School Redesign project. Along with the school redesign project, he hosts *Kansas Moonshot*, a podcast highlighting the amazing things educators are doing in their classrooms across the state of Kansas.

Josh has written for websites such as Edutopia, is a contributing author in *The Best Lesson Series: Literature*, and also writes on his blog, mrstockrocks.com. He does consultant work for Kansas University through a series of projects pairing technology with writing strategies.

Josh was selected as one of the National School Board Association's "20 to Watch" educational tech leaders in 2016, an International Society for Technology in Education Making IT Happen award recipient in 2017, an ISTE Emerging Young Educator award recipient in 2018, and an Outstanding Recent Graduate from Emporia State University in 2019.

ACKNOWLEDGMENTS

I am thankful to ISTE for giving me the opportunity to author this book and for Valerie Witte and Stephanie Argy for walking me through the process of publishing.

DEDICATION

Thank you to my wife, Jenica, for always believing in me, encouraging me to take risks, and supporting me in all my random ideas. And to our kids, Brooklyn and Oliver, for participating in all of my silliness, pausing vacations to record videos for the classroom, and being all-around amazing kids.

Thank you to my high school creative writing teacher, Ms. H, for helping me find my voice in my writing.

Thank you to Amber Rowland for mentoring me, encouraging me to share my ideas with others, and adding the term "Awesome Sauce" to my vocabulary.

Thank you to my mom for encouraging my writing and my dad for teaching me how to tell a great story.

Contents

TABLE OF *Awesomeness*

Introduction

You will fail.

For a book aimed at inspiring you, that is the worst opening line ever.

But failure is something you will run into. Making videos for your classroom is hard…as hard as trying to figure out the inner workings of a copier to unjam it! You set out to create the most amazing video, something Oscar-worthy or with an "O Captain! My Captain!" level of inspiration and awesomeness.

Then you run into an obstacle and you give up.

Even worse, you get so terrified about the possibility of messing up that you never even start. "It won't work." "Something will go wrong." You listen to the voices and don't create anything.

You will fail.

At some point in your video creation you will have issues. It won't be perfect. Things won't go exactly as planned. Your video will disappear, you'll stutter or mispronounce a word, or the school bell will interrupt an otherwise flawless recording.

Video creation is messy. Embrace it. Own it. I spent years talking myself out of some awesome ideas because I was afraid they wouldn't work. I would have an epiphany while on a walk or doing the dishes or taking a shower. Then I would sit down to plan out the next steps to make the creation a reality, and the doubt would creep in.

My biggest failure wasn't creating a messed-up video. It was being afraid to create anything in the first place.

Years ago, I created my very first video for my students. I spent hours meticulously recording and rerecording every second of footage for a short three-minute video. I thought the end result was great—until I showed it to students. As I watched it, I noticed a couple of "ummms" and a mistimed transition. All that work and there were still things that weren't perfect. That's when I decided not to worry so much.

Students love the mistakes. They love to see that you are human and struggle through things just like they do. I never knew the power of this connection until the time I received my first AirDropped image...of my face. I had sent out the daily announcement video on Google Classroom for students to watch before tackling the day's assignment. Ten minutes into the activity, a student AirDropped a screenshot from the video. In it, I was making the goofiest, weirdest face imaginable. Keep in mind that this was completely unintentional (sometimes I do goofy faces on purpose). It was hilarious, so I included it on my daily agenda the next day. For the next two weeks I had students poring through my videos trying to capture the goofiest Mr. Stock face.

In moments like this, you have two options. You can get frustrated and embarrassed that you sometimes look goofy when you make videos, or you can own it and use it to your advantage. The students didn't realize that while they were trying to find the screenshot gems in my videos, they were actually watching and rewatching my videos, engaged in learning the material.

You will fail. But you will bounce back from it. Continue moving forward and you will create something epic. You will create the Awesome Sauce—an epic video that keeps your students engaging with and mastering the content.

Setting the Table

Putting Together THE AWESOME SAUCE

I just finished my tenth year of teaching. Over that time, I've read hundreds of articles and books about teaching. I love learning new tools and tricks for the latest apps. I love being inspired to work with the most challenging students and encouraging them to *carpe diem*. I love the opportunity to explore new areas to grow. Some of the things I have read have been amazing and some not quite what I was looking for. The world of educational texts is overloaded with different genres, categories, and subcategories. However, it seems to boil down to two main approaches: the why and the how-to.

The *why* books are those educational books meant to inspire you to action, the books that send tingles down your spine and motivate you to be a better teacher. The *why* books are the keynote presentations of the educational world. They get you hyped up and ready to take on any challenge. A great *why* book makes you feel something and gets you ready to go and do something.

How-to books, on the other hand, give you real-world, step-by-step instructions for implementing a strategy or technology. A great *how-to* guides you through all the minute details that can help make implementation a resounding success. When you are ready to dive deep and get things going in your classroom, these are the books that get you jump-started. A great *how-to* book is like a great session you might attend at a conference: it tells you how to do something amazing in the classroom, laying the groundwork for the nuts-and-bolts systems that enable initiatives to roll out successfully.

Most books have some elements of both *why* and *how-to*, but ultimately they lean toward one end of the spectrum or the other. Each one has its merits and can help teachers move to the next level of awesomeness. An effective *why* book gets you so hyped up or emotionally invested that you want to move mountains to try to get things done—but a poor one will leave you with nothing but a scenic view. (I've finished the last page of many *why* books and had to ask myself, "Now what?") A great *how-to* book can provide the fundamental elements needed to go into your classroom the next day and implement something right away. However, *how-to* books can sometimes come across as sterile, with nothing that drives you to complete the steps they recommend.

Both types of books have a place in my tool box, and I find myself leaning more toward one or the other depending on my needs. Sometimes I want that reminder of why I do what I do, and other times I'm already hyped up and need a great set of action steps.

This book is intended to be a combination of *why* and *how-to*. Each chapter begins with the story of why I use the strategy. I want you to know why I bother putting effort into these activities. It requires a lot of work to try something new. I want you to see what you'll get out of trying the strategy. Along with each chapter is a set of *how-to* recipes to show you how to actually create the Awesome Sauce that your videos will become.

I hope that offering you the *why* and the *how-to* will help you create your own epic, Awesome Sauce videos!

THE *Awesome* SAUCE

Several years ago, Amber Rowland, a mentor of mine, encouraged me to share the cool things happening in my classroom with others. She brought me to my first ISTE conference as a co-presenter and encouraged me to present on my own at local conferences. When I was first starting out, she told me my videos were Awesome Sauce and that I needed to share them. I took that encouragement and started presenting about my Awesome Sauce videos at the Mid-America Association for Computers in Education conference (an ISTE affiliate).

Awesome Sauce is such a versatile phrase. It can serve various purposes: "You really brought the Awesome Sauce to that essay." "That was an Awesome Sauce presentation." "Bobby D's has the best Awesome Sauce for my BBQ sandwich." (That last one is just a reminder that I always bring the Awesome Sauce to my dad jokes.)

"Awesome" is a staple of my vocabulary. It is the foundation of my video catch-phrase—I wrap up every video by telling my students to "Book it forward and be awesome!"—so it made sense to make it the foundation of this book, too.

Bringing the Awesome Sauce is different for everyone. The beauty of video creation, like any other art form, is in the ability of the creator to infuse it with personality. The Awesome Sauce is that piece of YOU that you bring to the video: the creative spin, the nerdy hook that permeates your recordings. It is the reason your videos will be different from every other video created about your topic.

Awesome Sauce is a reminder to make every idea in this book your own. You know your students. You know your personality. You know the distinct thing that makes your classroom the highlight of a kid's day. If you can bring that into your videos, you will create something epic.

TECH *Know-How*

The goal of this book is to showcase a variety of ways to create Awesome Sauce videos in the classroom, regardless of what your tech skills are. I believe anyone with a smartphone, tablet, or any other recording device can create amazing videos for students. With a little creativity, even the most basic setups can yield great results.

The internet is littered with new technology elements that can spice up what you do, but don't let those distract or deter you from creating something epic. As you create, you will pick up tools and tricks along the way to improve and grow as a filmmaker. Watch plenty of YouTube videos and pay attention to how the YouTuber films different things.

A 2019 Common Sense Media census found that children ages 8–12 average about five hours of screen time daily, and teens about seven and a half hours—not including school or homework assignments! These two age groups also view an average of almost an hour of video content each day (Rideout & Robb, 2019). They are constantly immersed in online content.

Students love spending hours watching videos from the YouTube elite. Ask your students who their favorite YouTube celebrities are. Figure out why. Maybe they're not your style, but looking at popular YouTubers will give you some insight into what engages students.

This book doesn't dive too far into any technology specifics on purpose—the result of an eye-opening presentation I did to a group of teachers working on their master's degrees. I was sharing ways to integrate video into the classroom, using a presentation I'd done a dozen times before, but it had been six months since I had last shared it. Partway through my presentation, I had the teachers log onto Microsoft PowerPoint and try to download the Mix tab, only to find out that the Mix tab had gone away a couple of months earlier. That wasn't helpful. We ended up finding an alternative, but this reminded me that technology is dynamic. At the rate technology changes, anything I could put in this book would be outdated before it even goes to print. You'll find general ideas for technology and ways to use them, but for specific apps, websites, and tools connected to each recipe and section of this book, check out my website, mrstockrocks.com. There you'll find video tutorials and explanations that dive deep into the latest and greatest tools to accomplish what I outline in the book.

 To get started, check out the Awesome Sauce 101 playlist on YouTube: youtube.com/playlist?list=PLifJz8mRJxI3dCFS0jOCbR0e3JE2US094

WHY *Face Time* MATTERS

In college, I only had to take one math class. I've always been a decent math student and only needed to attend the test days to pass. I don't say that to brag—just to point out the bizarre nature of the class. I was "taught" through a series of online videos that went through the required curriculum. I have absolutely no idea who my instructor was.

I skimmed through most of it, maybe rewatching a video once if I really needed to. Other than that, the class wasn't helpful. In my classroom, I want the videos to feel like I am walking along with my students as they are learning. In an analysis of 6.9 million massive open online course (MOOC) video-watching sessions, Guo, Kim, and Rubin (2014) found that the most effective instruction videos incorporate some elements of the instructor speaking directly into the camera.

The internet is full of amazing video content I incorporate into my class. I still remember watching Bill Nye videos when I was a kid and being mesmerized by all the unique elements he introduced. There is nothing wrong with rocking some Bill Nye, but the majority of my videos have me in the video.

Videos in my classroom are an extension of myself. They are a means for me to be in a wide range of locations at one time. It's like cloning a not-quite-as-awesome version of myself. In a perfect world, I would sit down and work one-on-one with each of my students every single day. I would love to guide them through their learning journeys and help them any time they needed it. However, the reality is I have twenty-five to thirty kids in my room each day, and I have to do my best to distribute myself as best as I can.

It comes down to this: I want to be the best teacher possible, and using these recipes gives me the chance to make the biggest impact on the rock-star students in my classroom.

THE *Brain*

The brain is fascinating. It is a complex network of over 100 billion neurons linked together in an elaborate system (Herculano-Houzel, 2009). Scientists are constantly making new discoveries about how different parts of the brain interact. It is too complex a topic to cover in just a short section of this book, so I would highly encourage you to check out the articles referenced in the bibliography.

Cynthia Brame (2015) identifies three elements that are vital for video design and implementation to be effective: cognitive load, noncognitive elements that impact engagement, and features that promote active learning. This means that as you develop video content, you need to be aware of the strain placed on memory-storing processes, outside forces that might affect a viewer's understanding of the material, and elements you can add to make the video a more interactive experience.

Marcy P. Driscoll defines cognitive load as "the strain that is put on working memory by the processing requirements of a learning task" (2005). Have you ever tried to open up a YouTube video, download a large file from your e-mail, and work on a PowerPoint presentation while having ten or more tabs open on your internet browser? That's when you get the spinning icon or error message that lets you know something's not right. Your computer is trying to do too much and is overwhelmed by all of the processes it's trying to accomplish at one time. Your brain is like a computer in a lot of ways: If you overload its memory by trying to have it do too many things at once, it'll struggle to load new information. However, if information can be connected to prior schema, connections use less processing power and larger quantities of information can be processed at one time.

For new information to be stored indefinitely it needs to travel through three modes of memory.

1. **First, the learner uses *sensory memory* to determine which sensory signals deserve attention.** The learner is constantly bombarded with information. For example, when students sit down to watch a video, they are processing the sensation of the chair they're sitting in, the people around them, the posters on the wall, the case around the iPad, the pressure of the earbuds in their ears, and so on. All of these inputs are hitting the student, whose brain has to determine what is the most important, relevant information to focus on while tuning out the rest.

2. **Next, information filters through *working memory*, which has a limited capacity.** Your brain can only process four to five items in working memory at a time, and these stay in your brain for only around thirty seconds unless you do something with them. When I plan my videos for students, I try to present only one or two items of substantial information so as not to overload students' working memory.

3. **Finally, the information gets locked into *long-term memory* (Brame, 2015).** When you can connect new information to previous information, it goes into long-term memory. The more connections you can make to existing knowledge, the more likely it is that new information will stick.

Cognitive load theory analyzes how this network of systems interacts to create new learning. Three types of strain are placed on the brain in the process of learning: **intrinsic load**, which refers to the complexity of the learning task and the connections that are made between new learning and schema; **germane load**, which refers to the amount of working memory needed to support the intrinsic load; and **extraneous load**, which refers to any distractors that take away from the learning task (Brame, 2015).

Also important to consider when planning a video are the two channels of working memory: visual and auditory (Brame, 2015). When watching a video, students first process information with their sensory memory to determine what is relevant and important enough for working memory. They then have two channels to interpret information: auditory cues (sounds, voice-over, music) and visual cues (images, video, text on the screen). Too much text on the screen, voice-over without matching visuals, and music that overpowers the video can all overload the two channels, placing extraneous load on the learning task.

In their analysis of MOOC sessions, Guo, Kim, and Rubin (2014) found that the ideal video is less than six minutes long, includes periodic "talking head" scenes, and incorporates some of the techniques used in Khan Academy–style videos, especially the use of tablet drawings. Most important, the researchers found the quality of the video production did not have a direct impact on engagement.

Videos that rely too heavily on direct instruction and lecture can be ineffective because they lean too heavily on the audio channel of the brain and ignore the potential benefits of incorporating visual elements in the learning task (Thomson, Bridgstock & Willems, 2014). The most effective videos capitalize on both text and audio channels to demonstrate processes, tutorials, and other content by using visuals and music/narration (Thomson, Bridgstock & Willems, 2014).

John Hattie (2010) reviewed close to 1,200 meta-analyses to evaluate the effect size of over 250 instructional practices and the resulting learning outcomes. The higher the effect size, the greater the learning outcome: a practice that has an effect size of 0.4 will have an impact of one year's worth of growth over a school year and is what would be expected in a typical classroom. He found that interactive video has an effect size of 0.54 and micro-teaching/video review of lessons has an effect size of 0.88—both considerably higher than the standard yearly classroom effect size of 0.4, indicating that students learning from this method would show more than a year's worth of growth over the course of a year.

Ultimately, using videos successfully in the classroom comes down to balance:

1. including a balance of auditory and visual cues without overloading one side or the other;

2. maintaining a balance between new information and connections to old information; and

3. finding a balance between engaging and exciting content and content that overloads the learners.

Knowing how the brain is going to process your videos will help guide your video creations.

THE *ISTE* STANDARDS

The ISTE Standards for Educators and The ISTE Standards for Students are the guiding principles behind many of the ideas included in this book. The table below shows which recipes in the book support each ISTE Standard.

ISTE Standards for Educators

STANDARDS	VIDEO STRATEGY
2. Leader	Daily Announcements (ch. 2)
	Class Trailers (ch. 2)
	Beginning-of-the-Year Welcome Pack (ch. 2)
	School Tours (ch. 2)
	Video Introductions for New Students (ch. 2)
	Pep Talks (ch. 3)
	Classroom Recaps (ch. 3)
	Parent Updates (ch. 3)
	Anticipation Videos (ch. 4)
	Clarification (ch. 4)
	Video Edits (ch. 4)
	Screencasting Writing (ch. 4)
	In-Flipping (ch. 5)
	Test Review (ch. 5)
	Guided Reading (ch. 5)
	Test Accommodations (ch. 5)
	Physical Education Exercise Instructions (ch. 5)
	Meeting Updates (ch. 6)
	Substitute Plans (ch. 6)
	Technology Walkthroughs (ch. 6)
	Stop-Motion Videos (ch. 7)
	Characters (ch. 7)
	Travel Videos (ch. 7)
	Reading Recordings (ch. 8)
3. Citizen	Tweet Ups (ch. 3)
	Modified Socratic Circles (ch. 4)
	Public Service Announcements (ch. 8)

STANDARDS	VIDEO STRATEGY
4. Collaborator	Daily Announcements (ch. 2) Beginning-of-the-Year Welcome Pack (ch. 2) School Tours (ch. 2) Video Introductions for New Students (ch. 2) Pep Talks (ch. 3) Classroom Recaps (ch. 3) Parent Updates (ch. 3) Tweet Ups (ch. 3) Modified Socratic Circles (ch. 4) Meeting Updates (ch. 6) Substitute Plans (ch. 6) Technology Walkthroughs (ch. 6) Travel Videos (ch. 7) News Broadcasts (ch. 8) Student Recordings for Editing (ch. 8)
5. Designer	Beginning-of-the-Year Welcome Pack (ch. 2) School Tours (ch. 2) Station Instructions (ch. 4) Modified Socratic Circles (ch. 4) Scavenger Hunts (ch. 4) Gamification (ch. 4) Screencasting Writing (ch. 4)
6. Facilitator	Gamification (ch. 4) Goal Setting (ch. 8)
7. Analyst	Scavenger Hunts (ch. 4) Spelling Review (ch. 4) Gamification (ch. 4) Screencasting Writing (ch. 4)

ISTE Standards for Students

STANDARDS	VIDEO STRATEGY
1. Empowered Learner	Goal Setting (ch. 8) News Broadcasts (ch. 8) Student Recordings for Editing (ch. 8)
6. Creative Communicator	Rules for Next Year (ch. 8)
7. Global Collaborator	News Broadcasts (ch. 8) Student Recordings for Editing (ch. 8) Public Service Announcements (ch. 8)

CHAPTER

2

The Appetizer

(Part I)

The appetizer sets the tone for every amazing, memorable meal. It is the first thing you taste, and it whets your appetite for what's next. In schools, video lessons offered in the weeks leading up to the school year and during those first few days of school can be like appetizers, setting the tone for the rest of the year.

The videos in this section will help you get your year started on the right foot. If you're just starting out making videos, the first recipe below, Daily Announcements, is a great way to kick-start your video creation journey—and to set the tone for the school day.

Daily ANNOUNCEMENTS

POSSIBLE APPLICATIONS: Teacher to Student

The beginning of class is always hectic. I like to check in with students early on, but first I need to take attendance, and Kiera has a question about the writing assignment from last Thursday, and Oliver is crying because Brooklyn said something mean to him in the hall, and then I'm supposed to ask every student to attend the mixer after school today (at least, I think that's what the e-mail said—or was the mixer tomorrow?), and on top of that, I want to build a relationship with the quiet student who hasn't spoken the last few days. It's a lot to accomplish.

I used to start every class period by reading off class announcements—things like birthdays, assignment reminders, reading goals, and quotes of the day. As a middle school teacher, I was doing this for five classes a day. Every day. All that repetition was exhausting and felt like a waste of time, but I also knew that consistency was important for many of my students. I love to mix up seating arrangements and experiment with the structure of class activities, so announcements give us an anchor to start from, a calm, predictable moment before we launch into something amazing. (Offering routines like this is especially helpful for students who have executive functioning challenges.)

To make these announcements less exhausting, I decided to start recording them. I wanted a one-stop shop for all the most important events coming up, something I could show students at the start of class while I completed the usual beginning-of-the-hour tasks. The purpose of the video was to walk through this information once and then be able to reuse it for the rest of the day. And it worked great.

The first few times I did it, it took me about fifteen to twenty minutes to record the video because I kept restarting if I made a mistake. I wanted the video to be absolutely perfect. I noticed every "um" or "uh" or awkward pause. It was so time-consuming that I nearly gave up. But once I stopped worrying about perfection, I was able to get the time frame down to five to seven minutes for most of my announcement videos. I made a rule to limit myself to no more than three takes. Most days, I only needed one.

These videos freed me up to meet with individual students and complete administrative tasks, and they engaged the students a lot more than I would've just reading off upcoming due dates. Students pay more attention to a video than they would to me, because the videos are unique.

I also started to vary the way I presented information in the videos. Sometimes I would say a date for an assignment and have it written on the board behind me in the video; other times I would also point to the due date on the calendar. These variations were meant to engage different parts of students' brains.

My daily announcement videos usually follow the same general format:

1. First, I go through the daily announcements. These usually include upcoming assignments, reading checks, challenges, and anything else students may need to know in the near future. I always try to hold up a physical version of the actual assignment so they can visualize what I'm talking about.

2. Next, I do birthday announcements. I want to make sure every student who celebrates a birthday gets a shout out. I wasn't sure how important this was until I missed my first student, who was super bummed. Most students value this kind of positive affirmation, so anybody I miss always gets a special birthday shout-out the next day…usually with a guest like Batman. (To see what I mean by this, look at the Characters section in chapter 7.)

3. Finally, I wrap up the announcements video with the quote of the day. I have a chalkboard in my room where I always write a positive daily quote. Sometimes I just read the quote, and that's the end of the video. Other times I ask the students to talk about the quote when the video is over.

The last thing I include in my announcement videos is my catchphrase. Somehow it caught on and now the kids think it's weird if I don't end by saying "Until next time, book it forward and be awesome!"

DAILY ANNOUNCEMENT VIDEOS

Ingredients:

recording device (I usually just use my phone)

tripod (optional)

list of announcements

list of upcoming birthdays

Awesome Sauce

Prep Time: 2 to 5 minutes

Recording Time: 2 to 5 minutes

Difficulty: ● ○ ○ ○ ○

Directions:

1. Write down a list of the announcements you want to record; a bulleted list or script works. The more often you record these, the easier it will be to have a structure for what you want to include each time.

2. Find a location for the background of your video.

3. Gather any upcoming assignment materials or props you want to use in the video.

4. Set up your recording device.

5. Record an epic announcement video hitting all the main points for the day.

6. Post the video on YouTube.

7. Embed the video in your daily agenda slides, pull up the video on YouTube, or post the video for your students to view on their own time.

8. While students are watching the video, use the time to complete administrative tasks or check in with students.

Side note: To embed your YouTube video in Google Slides, go to Insert>Video. Then paste in the YouTube URL. To embed your YouTube video in Microsoft PowerPoint, go to the Insert tab, then Video>Online Movie. Then paste in the YouTube URL.

Check out this example: youtu.be/HRMKnEwe5S8

I share the videos in one of two ways. Sometimes I'll play the announcements on the big screen for all the students. Other times I'll share it on Google Classroom and let the students play it on their own.

To keep things interesting, I use variations from a lot of the other recipes in this book (see chapter 7 in particular for great ideas to incorporate into these videos).

CLASS *Trailers*

POSSIBLE APPLICATIONS: Teacher to Student

When I go to the movies, I love to get there early. I want to be in my seat with a large Pibb Zero and some popcorn, ready to roll when the first movie trailers pop up on the screen. I love the art of a great movie trailer. A good trailer will tell you what to expect when you go see a movie. A great trailer will make you count down the days until the movie comes out. An epic trailer will make you so excited for a movie that you go online to watch it three more times. Then you even research how many other versions of the trailer exist, and you try to watch all of those.

No trailers are more epic to me than the ones for Marvel movies. I'll watch the trailers online, then I'll search for follow-up information about the characters in them. From the heart-pounding music score to the action scenes to the comic relief, I love it all—and I want that same energy and hype for my classroom. I want my kids so excited for what's coming up in class that they repeatedly ask me when it's coming. I want them breaking down the doors to get into class. Class trailers can have that effect.

Every year when parents come to back-to-school night, I show a trailer promoting my class. This isn't just any trailer; it's a trailer for my gamified class, and it builds up all the energy, excitement, and chaos that is my class.

I preface the video by explaining the awards I've received, the articles and books I've written, and the conferences I've presented at—not to brag, but to assure parents that although my class is a little different, everything I do has a sound foundation to it. Then we roll into the trailer.

STUDENT-CREATED VIDEO

At the end of each unit, students can create a trailer highlighting everything they've learned. You can then use their trailers with your students the following year.

1. Brainstorm the most interesting elements from the unit.

2. Discuss how to build suspense and not give everything away.

3. Have groups of students write scripts based on the brainstorming.

4. Give the students time to record the video.

5. Select the best video(s) to use the following year.

CLASS TRAILERS

Ingredients:

background music

video snippets or photos of class

video-editing software

script

Awesome Sauce

Prep Time: 10 to 15 minutes

Editing Time: 45 to 60 minutes

Difficulty: ● ● ● ● ●

Directions:

1. Make a list of three to five things about your class that make it the most amazing, epic place any student will ever experience.

2. Choose what movie genre your class would be. (For example, is this a comedy or an action thriller?)

3. Find background music that fits your personality but also builds energy into the video. It should fit with your genre. (YouTube has library of free music for any video. Just search YouTube Audio Library or go to youtube.com/audiolibrary.)

4. Choose photos that fit with your genre and help tell the story.

5. Find or record video clips that help tell your story.

6. Edit your photos, video, and music together into a movie trailer with the Awesome Sauce. Keep it short, about one or two minutes.

7. Post your video on YouTube.

Share your video at back-to-school night, on your website, and on social media. You want every person who comes into your room to associate your class with the trailer.

Check out this example: youtu.be/psemCDR-LMg

The trailer starts out with an exciting rock track. This is vital to get everyone who watches the video hyped up and sucked into the video. The music rises to a crescendo, and a voice-over (which I attempt to read in the manner of a movie trailer narrator) explains the epic journey students will be embarking on in my class. It's just a taste of the meal that will come throughout the year. I also share the video with students, and they can't wait to start on the journey.

BEGINNING-OF-THE-YEAR *Welcome Pack* (WELCOME VIDEO/ROOM TOURS)

POSSIBLE APPLICATIONS: Teacher to Student

What if you could start shaping your future students' perceptions of your class before they ever set foot in your room? What if you could build up anticipation and excitement before the school year even starts?

When I was a kid, I had a few ways of knowing that summer was winding down. The first sign was our yearly pilgrimage to Walmart, school supply lists in hand. We would spend hours wandering aisle after aisle of tubs of crayons, shelves overflowing with crisp, clean backpacks emblazoned with superheroes, row after row of spiral notebooks with adorable kittens or Teenage Mutant Ninja Turtles, folders sporting the greatest athletes of the day, and of course every Lisa Frank product imaginable, items spilling off shelves and littering the floor. I loved all of it.

Another sign that signaled summer's end was the much-anticipated teacher reveal. I still remember being driven by my mom up the school's circular drive in our maroon Safari minivan and walking up to the front door where the school rosters were always posted. My brothers and I would frantically scan the lists with a mob of other anxious students, ready to whoop with joy or bow our heads in dread as we saw who we would be spending 180 days with in the near future. Once middle school hit, my friends and I would pore over our schedules trying to track down any and all information we could about our new teachers.

Every year around school registration, my team and I release our welcome website, welcometosft.weebly.com. It has everything an incoming sixth grader could want. There are links to videos that might interest the students, websites and games for the students to explore, photos from previous years showing exciting things students might get to participate in, and a video tour of the building.

In this way, students get to see video interviews with each of the team teachers, administrators, and counselors. Students want to see who they will be spending most of their time with. I want them to know our faces from Day One. I want them to know exactly who to go to if they need help during those first few days of school. A name on a schedule doesn't mean much, but kids are hooked if they see Mr. Stock talking about his class, hear the excitement in his voice, and find out about the spectacular things we might do.

CREATING A WELCOME VLOG

Ingredients:

recording device (I usually just use my phone)

tripod (optional)

Awesome Sauce

Prep Time: 1 minute

Recording Time: 2 to 5 minutes

Difficulty: ● ● ● ● ●

Directions:

1. Create a welcome website. This could be part of an existing website, but it should be a standalone site if possible. This is time-consuming the first year, but each year after that it's just a matter of updating the content. Check out my welcome website: welcometosft.weebly.com

2. Record a daily update starting in the middle of the summer.

3. Include things like the following:
   - sitting in the sun
   - enjoying family time
   - setting up your classroom (time lapse videos are fun for this)
   - any summer meetings you attend
   - the night before the first day of school

4. Post your video to YouTube.

5. Post a link to the video on your welcome website.

6. Repeat all summer leading up to the first day of school.

7. Share QR codes linking to the website on the front door of the school, in any welcome newsletters you send out, and anywhere else students and parents might see it.

Check out this example: youtu.be/b8-9lS2nt5g

Around mid-July, I start posting a video blog, or vlog, on the site. This leads up to the first day of school, and the goal is to build up excitement and suspense. I document everything going on at the school. I show videos of my room as it starts to come together. I share videos from meetings with the team to show how we are all in this together. I pull out books and do quick book talks to promote some of the exciting books students can borrow from my classroom library. All of these videos give students a feel for who we are. My goal is for the school to feel like a second home, and this is a small step toward meeting that goal.

SCHOOL *Tours*

POSSIBLE APPLICATIONS: Teacher to Student

Any time I'm in a new city or town, I love to explore. I love to go on adventures and discover hidden parks and restaurants. I hate crowds, so I like to avoid touristy areas if I can. But I'll be honest: I'm not a brave explorer. I do TONS of research before I go somewhere, looking up maps and videos of different parts of a city.

Students start their own adventure every year. New students are learning an entirely new building for the first time, and returning students may be exploring new parts of the building they never even knew existed. My school is a bizarre network of interlocking pods plus random hallway offshoots scattered throughout. It's fifty years old and has been remodeled over and over. It's a maze for experienced patrons—and a nightmare for newbies.

To alleviate student stress, I give video tours of the school. I share these with incoming sixth graders and students new to our team, but they can benefit anyone who is in the building for the first time. For my sixth graders, I give tours of the team classrooms, elective classrooms, the cafeteria, and the office. I also point out where a few of the best bathrooms are in the school. Students can watch the videos and visualize the school before they even arrive.

STUDENT-CREATED VIDEO

Students love to hear tips and tricks from other students. The older students know the best shortcuts, the hallways that are always congested, and the water fountains with the coldest water. Share tips for parts of the school students care the most about. Include a video for some of these areas:

1. **CAFETERIA.** What are students' favorite meals in the cafeteria? How do you get through the lunch line?

2. **LOCKER.** What are some tips for remembering locker combinations? What are some decorating tips?

3. **COUNSELING OFFICE/NURSE'S OFFICE.** Where can students get help if they need it?

4. **WATER FOUNTAINS/BATHROOMS.** Where are the nearest bathrooms? Which water fountains have the coldest water and the shortest lines? What is the school policy for hall passes?

SCHOOL TOURS

Ingredients:

recording device (I usually just use my phone)

tripod (optional)

map of the school

list of important locations (teachers in those locations if possible)

Awesome Sauce

Prep Time: 10 to 15 minutes

Recording Time: 30 to 45 minutes

Difficulty: ● ● ○ ○ ○
(more if you want to edit them together)

Directions:

1. Think about your audience. Who will be looking at these room tours? Plan out what school tour videos would be most beneficial for those audiences.

2. Make a list of every room you want to record and any hallway path that would be beneficial to know about.

3. For each room:

   a. Record the outside room door with the room number then walk inside.

   b. Record each room by doing a 360-degree turn inside it and explaining who is there.

   c. Try to come up with something unique for each room to help students remember it.

   d. Repeat for each room.

4. Record the hallway paths between rooms, especially those going from one important location to another, such as the path from the classroom to the cafeteria.

Check out this example: youtu.be/wsa9YJNdqfo

Imagine being a new student who transfers to a school. It's the middle of the year. Most of the students know exactly where to go. They are buzzing past this new student, who is lost and frustrated. Now imagine if this student watched a virtual tour of the building and knew exactly where to go on Day One. Imagine how that student is going to feel about your school. Or think of substitute teachers who are in the building for the first time; imagine how helpful they would find a quick video walkthrough.

VIDEO *Introductions* FOR NEW STUDENTS

At 9:30 a.m. on a Thursday, my students and I heard a knock on the door. I was in the middle of giving a life-changing speech; my students were perched on the edge of their seats, enthralled by my amazing words. (Okay, I was probably just saying something silly to get the class to laugh.)

One of my former students stood at the door with a student I had never met: "Uh, this is a new student. We're showing her around."

I tried to make the new student feel welcome, of course. I said "hi" and introduced her to the class before she continued her tour. But I could see the fear of starting a new adventure on her face.

I love meeting new students, and I'm glad they get to tour the school, but what if we looked at these tours differently? What if new students could watch a couple of quick videos to get to know their teachers before they even set foot in our classrooms? New students are already at a disadvantage because they have less experience with the adults in the building than the other kids. A quick peek in each of the rooms is great, but it doesn't come close to teaching new students everything they want to know.

We receive a lot of new students every year. Video introductions get them excited about school and give them a bit of comfort. Pair these with a video tour and they feel more confident about joining in with their new classmates. Videos let students see who's who among the teachers and practice teachers' names at home.

Parents of new students are also playing catch-up, and this tool gives them a jump start on their own journey, helping to build trust with the new

STUDENT-CREATED VIDEO

Being a new student can be scary. Starting off knowing someone right away can help. One way to make that happen is to form a welcoming committee of students who are assigned to make newcomers feel at home.

My team has a welcoming committee of about six students. On their first day, new students sit with one of the welcoming committee members to watch a one-minute video introducing the members of the committee. It's nothing fancy, just the students introducing themselves and letting the newbies know they can always ask them questions. Then the welcoming committee member walks the new student around the halls. Having several students in the video gives new students multiple opportunities to make new friends quickly.

VIDEO INTRODUCTIONS

Ingredients:

recording device (I usually just use my phone)

tripod (optional)

staff members

Awesome Sauce

Prep Time: 5 to 10 minutes

Recording Time: 30 to 60 minutes

Difficulty: ● ● ● ● ●

Directions:

1. Set up a time to interview all the people new students will interact with, including the following:

   - secretaries
   - counselors
   - librarians
   - nurses
   - principals
   - assistant principals
   - teachers

2. Record a quick introduction from each person (or have each person record a quick introduction and send it to you).

3. Post the videos on YouTube.

4. Host the recordings in one central location (e.g., a website) and create a one-page document with links or QR codes that new students can look over as needed.

5. As a bonus, record a video from the principal directly to parents and include a link to it on a welcome letter that goes home the first day.

Check out this example: youtu.be/ilODkPnv5yE

adults in their children's lives. Transitions are tough for anyone, and the faster the student-teacher-parent connections can click, the faster learning can take place. Trust is a necessary foundation for learning content, and introductory videos help to develop it.

3

The Appetizer
(Part II)

A positive classroom climate is the foundation for great learning. This fundamental element can transform a student's interpretation of the importance of school. The videos in this chapter provide opportunities to create a positive learning environment where students feel valued.

Pep TALKS

POSSIBLE APPLICATIONS: Teacher to Student

Every sports movie ends the same way: At halftime, the team (a perennial underdog, of course) is losing, with no hope of winning the big game against their fiercest rival. Every player has given up hope. Heads are bowed; sometimes players are punching lockers or yelling at one another. Then someone steps forward out of the crowd and gives the speech of a lifetime. Sometimes it's the coach, sometimes the captain of the team, sometimes that player you never expect. This person sums up how the team has changed, how they just need to come together, and how they are going to destroy the other team. They are the greatest, the best there ever was. Nobody will ever defeat them again!

That momentum, that inspirational moment that gets you fired up to tackle a challenging task, is why I love to create my own pep talk videos. For everything from a state assessment to a big project presentation to a robotics competition, these videos give students an extra boost.

The videos also serve as great front-end interventions and positive reinforcement tools. They help build a stronger classroom (and sometimes schoolwide) community and could easily become a part of a Positive Behavior Interventions and Supports (PBIS) by laying out clear goals for the upcoming challenge.

I've made pep talk videos in different ways:

1. One of my favorite approaches is to go around to all the teachers and administrators in the building and have them wish the students good luck. Having every adult in the building in the video shows students we are all in this together. Most students have that one adult who always has their back or who understands them better than anyone else. Having everyone in the video reminds them of that connection, and makes it feel like the teachers are talking directly to them.

2. I also like to invite "guests" to wish students good luck. For more on this, check out the recipe about characters in chapter 7.

3. Anytime I'm on vacation somewhere like the beach, I try to record a pep talk video so that students can visualize themselves in a calming place when they are tackling a difficult task.

4. I also love a simple "good luck" from the heart. Sometimes the simplest videos, reaffirming that you believe in your students and reminding them that they are amazing, can have a huge impact.

PARENT-CREATED VIDEO

Sometimes videos are even more meaningful if you involve parents. It's always a surprise for students, and parents love to be involved. Consider recording good luck videos from parents at parent-teacher conferences. You can do this a few ways:

1. Have a recording device ready. At the end of the conference, ask the parents to say a quick good luck to the student as you film them. (Alternatively, you could make a more general good luck video for the class featuring a montage of a lot of different parents.)

2. Type instructions on how to share a video on a flier and ask parents to send one in when they get home. This is trickier than the first option, because parents aren't always reliable about sending things in. (I say this as a parent who would probably forget to send it in.)

3. Have a station set up outside the room where parents can go and record a quick good luck video after they finish the conference. In this case, make sure to have plenty of instructions on how to record the video.

This also works for rules videos: you could have parents record a quick video reading your classroom rules at back-to-school night, then edit the video to show each parent sharing one rule. You could even have a series of these videos and rotate them throughout the year. The more you show students they have a circle of people who want them to succeed and are actively engaged in their education, the better.

PEP TALK

Ingredients:

recording device (I usually just use my phone)

tripod (optional)

video-editing software

guests

background music

Awesome Sauce

Prep Time: 10 to 15 minutes

Recording Time: 10 to 60 minutes (depending on how many guests you include)

Difficulty: ● ● ● ● ●

Check out this example: youtu.be/ICKbsuflqQY

Directions:

1. Set up a time to meet with every adult in the building with whom your students interact.

2. Have each person wish the students good luck on video. If you keep the language somewhat generic, you can then use this video for multiple occasions. Encourage each person to keep it short.

3. Edit the clips together into one video using your editing software of choice. I use iMovie on my iPad or Camtasia on my computer. Include introduction text, transitions between each person, and concluding text with the words "Good Luck!" in big bold letters to make sure that's the last thing students see.

4. For bonus hype, add pump-up music. (YouTube has a library of free music for any video. Just search YouTube Audio Library or go to youtube.com/audiolibrary/)

5. Don't post the video anywhere until *after* you show it to your students—it makes for a great surprise. I usually either show it on the big screen before the activity I want them hyped up to tackle or I share it on Google Classroom for all of them to see on their own devices.

CLASSROOM *Recaps*

POSSIBLE APPLICATIONS: Teacher to Student

"How was school today?"

"Fine."

"What did you learn today?"

"Stuff."

Parents across the country have this exact same conversation almost every day. That's where the class recap comes into play. One of the most powerful videos I create for students is the end-of-the-day wrap-up video in which I recap what we covered for the day and update students on anything that needs to be completed for the next day.

The beauty of recording this video at the end of the day is twofold.

First, it lets me review what we actually accomplished for the day. Every day I have a long list of things I would like to cover. I have activities to complete, challenges to roll out, the occasional dice battle to referee. I have so much to do that it's nice to reflect on what we've missed—and it also gives me a good jump start on the next day's planning.

Second, I post all of these videos on YouTube. Parents who subscribe to my channel have a quick peek into my classroom and can pick up some great talking points for the dinner table. Instead of asking "How was your day?" parents can ask "Did you enjoy pretending to climb up Mt. Everest today?" or "What did you think about Rosa Parks' bravery in standing up for what she believed in?" I understand that parents are busy and don't always have time to watch the videos, but they can access them any time they need a good dinner table topic.

The wrap-up videos give parents and students a chance to reflect on the awesomeness that is Room 508.

STUDENT-CREATED VIDEO

As the year goes on, I try to include students in the process more and more. For instance, I like to invite them to join me in my videos summarizing what we accomplished each day. (That's always a shocking experience: sometimes it lets me know that students valued something completely different than I had expected.) Involving students in the videos makes sense because kids are more likely to watch videos if their classmates are in them, so in the last five minutes of class I'll pull a couple of students out into the hall and have them recap what we learned for the camera. Sometimes I use all the videos; other times I only use the best one. I then post these videos on YouTube, Google Classroom, and Instagram.

CLASSROOM RECAPS

Ingredients:

recording device (I usually just use my phone)

tripod (optional)

bulleted list of topics covered and due dates

Awesome Sauce

Prep Time: 2 to 5 minutes

Recording Time: 5 to 10 minutes

Difficulty: ● ● ● ● ●

Check out this example: youtu.be/o89-CscHgz0

Directions:

1. Make a list of upcoming due dates.

2. Make a list of the most important topics/ideas covered today.

3. Record a video going through reminders about important due dates and the most important topics covered.

4. Wrap up with a positive statement. Let kids know they are awesome!

Post the video on YouTube and any other social media feeds you use.

PARENT *Updates*

POSSIBLE APPLICATIONS: Teacher to Parents, Administrator to Parents

The year my daughter started kindergarten was a truly eye-opening experience. Until then, I had only experienced teacher-parent interactions from a teacher's perspective. I would get frustrated when parents wouldn't follow up on e-mails or notes I sent home with the students. I didn't understand why parents were confused by due dates or classroom policies. Didn't they take the time to read the detailed syllabus I included in the welcome packet?

Then I went to my daughter's first registration event. Let me preface this by saying that my daughter goes to a spectacular elementary school. The staff there truly care about each student and want to make sure students are pushed to reach their fullest potential. But when I walked into the front entrance of the school, I wasn't prepared for what awaited me. First, I received a paper outlining all the different extracurricular activities students could choose to join.

Then I went to another table and received a flyer for spirit wear, then an allergies flyer from the nurse, then lunch schedules, then school supplies lists. By the end of registration, I had a stack of papers that, to be honest, I went through quickly, keeping the two things I thought I might need and recycling the rest.

Over the past four years, I have received enough flyers, e-mails, and documents from my daughter's school to wallpaper a large room. I understand why they do it: this information is vital, and it's important to inform parents about things that are coming up. However, it can also be overwhelming. I can't imagine what it will be like next year when my son starts school and the paperwork doubles!

Yet as a teacher, I still send home stacks of papers and flyers, and I don't intend to stop anytime soon. I send home the welcome packet and the newsletters, and plenty of parents use the paper versions. However, to help parents who just want a quick overview of important events coming up, I've also started making videos (although I don't send them out often—usually only when big events are coming up).

The videos usually start with a big thank-you. My job is immensely easier when parents support schoolwork at home, so I want to thank them for all they do to help me.

Next, I throw out a quick list of the most important due dates, field trips, and school activities—emphasis on MOST IMPORTANT. If the robotics team has practice on Wednesday night, I can talk to those kids' parents directly. I just want to give them the CliffsNotes version of what's coming up in Room 508.

STUDENT-CREATED VIDEO

Bring students in to record the parent update videos, giving them a list of important information to read on camera. Parents love to see their kids discussing what's going on in class, and they are a lot more likely to pay attention in case this is the week their baby makes it into the video.

These videos also help parents put a face to a name. They have enough going on without needing to stress over remembering who their kid's teacher is. But I want them to be able to recognize me if we run into each other at the grocery store. They entrust me with their children, the most important thing in their life. Parents can do that more easily when they can see the teacher's face, hear the energy in what the teacher is saying, and perceive that the teacher truly loves their job.

PARENT UPDATE VIDEOS

Ingredients:

recording device (I usually just use my phone)

tripod (optional)

list of upcoming events and MOST IMPORTANT information

Awesome Sauce

Prep Time: 2 to 5 minutes

Recording Time: 5 to 10 minutes

Difficulty: ● ● ● ● ●

Directions:

1. Don't overdo this!
2. Find a time when parents need super important information (upcoming field trips, monthly newsletters, big assignments coming up, etc.).
3. Make a list of important things to cover.
4. Record a very succinct video.
5. Post the video on YouTube.
6. Share the video with parents.

Side Note: I usually include a print version of the information in the video for parents who would rather read the information.

Check out this example: youtu.be/SRvucuvAMss

Parents have given me a lot of positive feedback about these videos. They like how simple they are. They can watch them quickly instead of wading through a stack of papers.

I want to speak directly to each and every parent and tell them that I love their kids, that we have amazing things coming up in the class, and that I'm there if they have any questions. Since I can't always do that in person, I use videos. That's how you roll out the Awesome Sauce.

Tweet UPS

People can be mean. It's as simple as that. Adults or kids, it doesn't matter. They can say mean, hurtful things that can tear down the students who walk through my doors. And that's not even including the negative self-talk.

I teach in a middle school, that time when students are transitioning from children into teenagers. It's awkward and sometimes goofy and embarrassing.

Students can easily build up a negative idea of who they are and let others define who they will become. To counter that, I'm constantly trying to find ways to build up my students. I tell them why they're awesome and try to encourage them any way I can. But sometimes that isn't enough, because my words don't hold the same weight as those of their peers.

I came up with the idea of Tweet Ups to combat this problem. Tweet Ups are little slips of blue paper meant to look like tweets from Twitter that students use to write positive messages to each other. The kids get a chance to put some positivity into the world, tell their classmates why they rock, and show them they aren't going unnoticed.

Here's how it works. On one of my shelves, I keep a box in which students can put completed Tweet Ups. Once a week, I pull out all the Tweet Ups and read them in a special edition of my daily announcement video. The students love hearing Tweet Ups about themselves and their classmates (not to mention sneaking in some inside jokes).

Tweet Ups help create a classroom culture of building up others. They serve as a great front-end intervention to reinforce positive behaviors in the classroom. Students get positive recognition from their peers, which encourages them to continue the positive behavior, and other students emulate those positive behaviors so that they too can be recognized—a loop of positivity.

STUDENT-CREATED VIDEO

After students get used to writing their Tweet Ups, I like to bring volunteers in to read their Tweet Ups on video. This reduces the awkwardness that some middle schoolers feel giving or receiving compliments face to face. I usually have students stop by after school and record their Tweet Ups. It takes five minutes. I still have them fill out the Tweet Up form, which I then post on my Wall of Awesome.

Students can take credit for writing a Tweet Up or they can keep it anonymous. The nice thing about anonymous Tweet Ups is that I can write some about great things kids are doing, and they don't know it's from me. Sometimes it's better if it sounds like it came from one of their peers.

About halfway through the year, I usually ask if anyone would like a list of students who haven't received a Tweet Up yet. A handful of students take the challenge and make sure every single student gets recognized. I'm always cognizant of the need for tact on this. I don't want students to feel embarrassed about

EPIC TWEET UP VIDEOS

Ingredients:

recording device (I usually just use my phone)

tripod (optional)

intro music

Tweet Up pages

box for the Tweet Ups

Awesome Sauce

Prep Time: 2 to 5 minutes

Recording Time: 3 to 7 minutes

Difficulty: ● ● ● ● ●

Directions:

1. Have a place in the classroom where students can get Tweet Up pages and a box where they can turn them in.

2. Once a week, take all the Tweet Ups out of the box.

3. Record a video reading the Tweet Ups.

4. At the end of each video, add a reminder about how to write more Tweet Ups.

5. Post the video on YouTube.

6. Share the Tweet Ups with students.

Optional: Add a theme song to the Tweet Ups—even better if it's student-created.

Optional 2: Make a list of students who haven't had a Tweet Up yet this year. Share it with specific students who might be interested in writing some extras—or share it with everyone!

Check out this example: youtu.be/f1h0NH9PgT4

Check out this Tweet Up PDF: drive.google.com/file/d /1TY7PofJ4HtEslKvCz8eJH7MANV6cCoCL/view?usp=sharing

not receiving a Tweet Up yet, and I also don't want them to feel like their Tweet Up is insignificant. So far everything has worked out perfectly.

Once the Tweet Ups have been read, I hang them on the Wall of Awesomeness celebrating the unique ways students bring the Awesome Sauce every day. When the bulletin board is full or at a good transition time (during winter break, for example), I take down all the Tweet Ups and hand them out. It amazes me how many students keep the Tweet Ups in their binder for the rest of the year.

(By the way, I can't take full credit for Tweet Ups: my wife originally designed the form I use for her fifth-grade classroom.)

4

The Main Course
(Part I: Engagement)

For students to learn in the classroom, they need to be actively engaged in exploring the content. These videos help get students engaged in class and keep them hooked in a variety of ways. Some of the videos here will better reach different learning styles and provide students with more self-paced instruction.

Anticipation VIDEOS

POSSIBLE APPLICATIONS: Teacher to Student

One day last year, I knew I would be out of the classroom for an appointment. I also knew we were wrapping up our most recent unit, and I wanted to prep the students for the next one. A couple of years before, I had attended a professional development session with Dave Burgess, author of *Teach Like a Pirate*, who called this type of prep "preheating the grill." To grill a steak, you have to preheat your grill—you want it primed so the steak sizzles when you throw it on there. I wanted to create a sizzle around our next unit.

Over the years, I've led my students through a wide range of activities to get them interested in an upcoming lesson. We've "flown" on a plane to Tibet for our reading of *Peak* by Roland Smith. We've discussed wilderness survival techniques before diving into the novel *Hatchet* by Gary Paulson. The students completed a survey and had an intense Socratic Circle over what makes the best leader.

One of the first times I attempted a video to build up some anticipation, I made a bold and risky choice. My goal was to make a video that would capture the students' attention, provoke a strong reaction, and get them to think. I recorded the video and posted it on Google Classroom for the students to watch before they started working. In the video, I made my regular announcements, then dropped this bomb: "There's one thing that's been bothering me. I don't think girls should be allowed to be firefighters. They're just not strong enough." Then I listed all the jobs I thought girls weren't strong enough for.

Whoa! Did THAT get the students fired up! Within five minutes of class starting, I got angry e-mails from some girls in class. I responded by telling them to watch the rest of the video, where I said that I didn't truly believe those statements and explained the problem with stereotypes in general. I added that we would be discussing gender roles and stereotypes and the role of society in shaping them.

The next day, students took a survey in which they rated on a 1–5 scale how much they agreed or disagreed with the statements in the video. Then we had a Socratic Circle to discuss the statements. The video sparked a lot of interest and led to a rich, engaging discussion. All I had to do was step back and watch in amazement.

ANTICIPATION VIDEOS

Ingredients:

recording device (I usually just use my phone)

tripod (optional)

position statement(s)

Awesome Sauce

Prep Time: 5 to 7 minutes

Recording Time: 5 to 10 minutes

Difficulty: ● ● ● ● ●

Check out this example: youtu.be/6VPT-E4LQXM

Directions:

1. Write a script or at least a bulleted list of things that have "really been bothering you."

2. Start recording the video.

3. Share some statement connected to your content that you know will get students' attention. There's a fine line you'll have to walk for this one. You don't want to go too far—some statements are off-limits. I always run these ideas by several trusted colleagues who will give me honest feedback.

4. If you'd like, record a disclaimer at the end of the video. Sometimes I don't and just let the attention-grabbing statement sit there until the next day.

5. Post the video on YouTube.

6. Share the video with students.

After some reflection, I realized that the outcome was good, but the approach was problematic. This is one of the trickiest forms of student engagement. If I were to recreate that video again, I would start by changing the statement to "some people argue that girls aren't strong enough to be firefighters. What do you think?" And then I would explain that we would be having a discussion the next day where they would have the opportunity to express their views.

A quick anticipation video can go a long way toward getting students interested in what's coming up. It encourages them to think through their beliefs about an idea and gets them engaged in a topic before they even get to class. Most importantly, it makes kids want to come to school to see what will happen next.

Clarifications

POSSIBLE APPLICATIONS: Teacher to Student

I have a confession to make: when I have a substitute, I may stalk my students' Google Docs. It's not that I don't trust the amazing subs who come into my classroom, although I have had a couple who've gone off script. I just want to know what the students are working on. (I do the same thing when I'm in the room with the students too, so it's not that creepy, right?)

Let's just call it "monitoring." I monitor the students' Google Docs to check for understanding. I like to do a quick check-in to see when they start typing. If they take a long time getting started, it usually means they experienced some sort of technical difficulty, although it could also mean they were off task. I also look for confusion—a student starting to type something and then erasing it, for example. Honestly, sometimes I monitor their Docs just to mess with them. The first time I start typing on one of their Docs because they are off task is awesome! They're usually shocked, then quickly realize they need to get back to work.

During one of these monitoring sessions, I figured out that my students were confused over a writing assignment I had posted on Google Classroom. Sitting in the dentist's office waiting for my daughter to finish her appointment, I watched student after student write responses that were not even close to what I had intended. I knew I needed to do something to correct it.

My daughter finished getting her pearly whites cleaned, and I dropped her off at her school. In the parking lot, I looked over a couple of assignments from students at various ability levels to see if everyone was confused or if it was just a select group. Every single student was making the same mistakes. To correct this, I pulled out my phone and started recording. I explained where students were getting stuck and a couple of suggestions for how to improve the assignment. I loaded it up on YouTube and then posted it on Google Classroom. Within seven minutes, I had corrected the assignment for the rest of the students that day—from the parking lot of my daughter's school.

I still had to go back and reteach my first two classes of students, but this saved a lot of struggle for my last two classes. The next day, students told me the video helped a lot. I even had a few students from the first two classes who watched the video when they got home and corrected the assignment on their own. That's the

CLARIFICATIONS

Ingredients:

recording device (I usually just use my phone)

tripod (optional)

screencast software

microphone

Awesome Sauce

Prep Time: 2 to 5 minutes

Recording Time: 5 to 10 minutes

Difficulty: ● ● ● ● ●

Directions:

1. Decide what type of correction this is. If it's a quick-fix video, go to step 2. If it's a more intensive correction, go to step 9.

2. Record a video of you walking the students through the assignment again.

3. If the assignment is on paper, hold it up. If it's digital, remind students where to access it.

4. Emphasize sections that seemed particularly confusing.

5. Make sure to highlight that many students struggled. Take some of the responsibility for this.

6. Post the video on YouTube.

7. Share the video with students through Google Classroom or some other means.

8. Done.

9. Complete steps 1–8, only record an entire screencast (or a recording of your computer screen, instead of just a video of you) walking through the places where students struggled. An alternative is to write the assignment yourself and narrate what choices you make through the process.

Check out this example: youtu.be/T1kB1ZT0UlA

magic of pairing correction videos with learning management tools like Google Classroom. I can connect with my students even when I'm not there.

On another occasion, I was grading an essay and I noticed that my students completely lost track of what they were supposed to do. I realized I had done a terrible job showing them how to effectively use evidence in their writing. This was a much bigger issue than a quick three-minute video could fix. Instead, I recorded a new video, which was a screencast of me walking through every step of the essay I wanted students to write. I talked through the choices I was making and emphasized how I chose the evidence I wanted to use. I then uploaded the screencast to YouTube and posted it and the writing to Google Classroom.

The next day I had the students use a split screen to watch the video on one half and read their essays on the other half. I had them look for places where they needed to improve their use of evidence. While they watched the video and jotted down notes, I was able to walk around and conference with individual students. The video showed them how I would approach the essay. If they were stuck, they could follow my lead. Once the students were back on solid ground again, they were able to branch out on their own path to complete their essays.

This is just one of many ways to use videos to model writing for students. Modeling how I want the students to complete a task gives them a guide to follow when they are lost. It acknowledges that I see their struggle and it gives them the tools to fix their confusion. It gives them the power to solve their problems. A video can provide everything from a quick adjustment to a lengthy walk-through of a problem in a timely way.

Station INSTRUCTIONS

POSSIBLE APPLICATIONS: Teacher to Student

One of the most difficult parts of teaching is that no matter how hard I try, I can't be everywhere at once. I'll be working with one student to troubleshoot a problem with her essay, then two other hands shoot up. By the time I get to those two other students, three more students aren't sure what to do next. It gets to be exhausting. I bounce around like a confused superball and never give my full attention to the students who need it most.

STUDENT—CREATED VIDEO

Students love hearing from older kids. The younger kids look up to the older ones for advice (as long as they're not siblings). Sometimes I'll pull in some of my former students and have them record videos. This works best if the students are at least two grades older and are still at the same school. This way the kids can recognize them in the halls after they watch the videos.

I love using stations and rotations to ease the strain of trying to be everywhere at once. I've been doing this for years. Stations are nothing new, but video instructions have transformed my rotation time. When I first started my teaching career, rotation days were just like any other day, with me repeating the same instructions over and over and over again. I tried

ROTATION INSTRUCTION VIDEOS

Ingredients:

recording device (I usually just use my phone)

tripod (optional)

station scripts

project samples (optional)

QR creator website (e.g., qr-code-generator.com)

printer

Awesome Sauce

Prep Time: 10 minutes per station

Recording Time: 5 to 10 minutes per station

Difficulty: ● ● ● ● ●

Check out this example: youtu.be/98CaldoxFFs

Directions:

1. Write out the instructions for each station in a script to ensure you don't leave out anything important.

2. Create any samples of what the students will be doing. Sometimes it helps for them to see what the finished product should look like.

3. Record a video for each station with instructions. Make sure the camera is set up with enough distance to get everything in the frame.

4. Upload each video to YouTube.

5. Copy the URL for each YouTube video and paste it onto a QR generator website.

6. Depending on the QR generator site, you will either download the QR code or use a screen-capture tool to take a picture of each QR code. Make sure when you save the QR code you name the file in a way that will allow you to easily find it.

7. Attach the QR code to the bottom of the typed instructions. Include both the QR code and written instructions at each station. Some students like to read the instructions while watching the videos.

explaining all the stations at once, but students would only pay attention to the station they were going to next. Then I tried having written instructions on the table. This worked for some students, but students who struggle with reading had trouble—or wouldn't even bother starting on the instructions.

Then the "Aha!" moment hit. I recorded a video for each of my stations explaining exactly how to approach it. In some of the rotations, I included demonstrations of how to complete a task. Then I would pull up the videos on YouTube on a laptop at each rotation. Students could watch and rewatch the instructions as many times as necessary until they completed the task. When they rotated to the next station they could repeat the process.

Now that we are a 1:1 iPad school, it's even easier. I can have the students scan a QR code and watch the videos on their devices, as a group or on their own. It saves time and energy.

The videos allow students autonomy over their learning. Adding flexibility about which stations students work at gives students the opportunity to learn in a style that best meets their needs.

Book TALKS

POSSIBLE APPLICATIONS: Teacher to Student, Student to Student

Books have always been a huge part of my life. Ever since I was a little kid, I've always had a book close by, and I'm usually juggling five or six in various drop spots in my house. This has always served me well as a language arts teacher. One of the best parts of my job is getting the chance to share great books with students. I love seeing that fire ignite when they get hooked on a great book. I love hearing them talk about a book we've both read and seeing the excitement they get when they get to be active members of that conversation. Most of all, I love being able to help shape the reading lives of my students.

STUDENT-CREATED VIDEO

Students are even better at doing book talks than adults, because they know what their friends enjoy. They can point out things I would never think of and make references to pop culture I can't keep up with. Challenge students to create a book talk about their favorite book. Give them a quiet space to record. If you want to take it to the next level, you could add a green background and allow the student to play around with some green screen effects. The most important thing is for the student to have the book in their hand when they are recording. Students need a visual of the book cover to help them find it in the library.

As surprising as this will sound, not all kids like fantasy or science fiction books. Who knew that people read other genres? Actually, I do branch out from time to time, and I have a handful of books I love to share with kids in each genre. Once they have read my small selection of book recommendations for books with a middle-school girl protagonist (I'm a big fan of the book *How to Rock Braces and Glasses* by Meg Haston), I'm out. All I can do is direct students to other students who like the same kinds of books.

That's where other teachers can make a huge difference. Book talks from

BOOK TALKS

Ingredients:

recording device (I usually just use my phone)

tripod (optional)

teachers

recommended books

QR code generator

Awesome Sauce

Prep Time: 5 to 10 minutes

Recording Time: 30 to 45 minutes

Difficulty: ● ● ● ● ●

Check out this example: youtu.be/GB-QzK8j0oA

Directions:

1. Send out an e-mail to staff asking for their book recommendations.

2. Ask each teacher who responds if they would be willing to record a video of that book recommendation.

3. Set up a time to record the video.

4. Record the video. Make sure the teacher is holding the book in the video and that the title and author are both mentioned.

5. Post the video on YouTube.

6. Create a QR code of the video.

7. Print off copies of the QR code, put them on bookmarks, and put the bookmarks in the book.

8. Create a poster in the library with a picture of the teacher and a list of the book talk videos.

teachers around the school can show even reluctant readers that there might be a place for reading in their lives. Kids who love sports might not care about my recommendation, but they might pick up a book their coach recommends.

Other teachers not only have knowledge in areas I don't, they may also connect with students in different ways than I do. Give me a group of students who love to play Dungeons & Dragons or can name all the actors who have donned the Robin costume, and I can find stacks of books for them. Those are the ones who seem to click with me. Each student has a go-to person in the building. I'm okay with not being that person for every student. My job is to track down that person for my students and get some good book recommendations from them.

We've done teacher suggestion cards in our library to get kids interested in books. They can find a book recommended by a teacher they love and check it out. That teacher has a lot of credibility with that student. Now, imagine taking it to the next level and having that teacher not only write down a book they love but also record a video explaining why they loved it. Seeing a teacher's face when they recommend something makes it feel like they are talking directly to you.

MODIFIED *Socratic* CIRCLES

POSSIBLE APPLICATION: Student to Student

Shocker: Students love to argue. They love to explain why they are right and everyone else is wrong. Unfortunately, they don't always have great tact when it comes to discussions like this. I like guiding students through the process of an intelligent, thought-provoking discussion where everyone has a voice and everyone respects and listens to the rest of the group. We work together on learning to engage with a group when we disagree while still being able to walk away as friends. It's a skill that many adults would benefit from as well.

To help students through this process, I use Socratic Circles. A Socratic Circle is a strategy for having students engage in a dialogue. Students sit in two circles, an inner circle and an outer circle. The inner circle talks about a topic for a certain amount of time while the outer circle observes, takes notes on the content of the conversation, and sometimes analyzes the quality of the discussion.

To begin the discussion, I usually give the class an article or survey. We also spend a lot of time prepping for how to contribute appropriately to a discussion, how to engage everyone in the group, and how to disagree appropriately. After the time is up, we reflect on the discussion and the groups switch places.

I love this method of discussion. However, it doesn't always allow the quieter students an entry point into the conversation, especially at the beginning of the year. Some kids, like some adults, love to hear themselves speak and don't always know when to cede the floor to someone else.

Modified Socratic Circles can help with this problem. In this version of the strategy, students record a video response to the article or discussion topic. Then they watch all the videos and post their own video responses to those videos. They can finish up by making responses to the responses.

The great thing about this approach is it gives viewers a chance to think about their responses before they record them. The discussion still has the nuances of conversation that a chat or discussion board loses.

MODIFIED SOCRATIC CIRCLES

Ingredients:

recording devices

microphones if needed

article for discussion

site to post the videos

Awesome Sauce

Prep Time: 5 to 10 minutes

Recording Time: 10 to 15 minutes

Difficulty: ● ● ● ● ●

Directions:

1. The day before, give all students a copy of the article for discussion. Have them mark up the text according to whatever annotation strategies your school uses.

2. Have each student show you their article on the way into class. Students who haven't marked up the text can work on finishing that up.

3. Students who are finished will record a video responding to the text by pointing out something they agreed with, something they disagreed with, or a question they have.

4. Students will post their recordings to a shared location, whether it's a shared Google Drive folder, Google Classroom, or something else.

5. Students will then watch videos from their classmates and post responses to those videos.

6. The first time you do this, go over how to appropriately disagree with a classmate and how to use evidence effectively. Give plenty of examples as well.

Check out this example: youtu.be/HA11wAkh9S0

SCAVENGER *Hunts*

POSSIBLE APPLICATIONS: Teacher to Student, Administrator to Teachers

When I was little, I loved to go on secret quests. I would draw treasure maps on tattered notebook paper covered in dirt with an X marking the spot for the golden pirate booty. (I also thought it was hilarious that it was called "booty.") I would make these maps for my brothers, too, and force them to search the backyard for treasures (often just their own toys that I had hidden).

STUDENT-CREATED VIDEO

Kick the scavenger hunt up another notch by having students create video responses to the clues. Here are some examples:

1. Record a video acting out a scene from the novel the class read.

2. Record a video with a group member explaining the difference between revolving and rotating using at least two objects in the room. Another group member must be revolving or rotating in the video.

3. Record a video demonstrating the difference between perimeter and area using only the objects found on the table.

SCAVENGER HUNT

Ingredients:

recording device (I usually just use my phone)

tripod (optional)

clues

QR code videos

Awesome Sauce

Prep Time: 45 to 90 minutes

Recording Time: 10 to 15 minutes

Difficulty: ● ● ● ● ○

Check out this example: youtu.be/P6Xxa9HZXoQ

Directions:

1. Choose the content you want to deliver with the scavenger hunt.

2. Choose a theme for the hunt.

3. Create five to ten clues that lead to the next location in the hunt. Each clue should be connected to the theme and help tell the story.

4. The last clue should have a mega challenge to wrap up the activity.

5. Record a video for each clue.

6. Post each video on YouTube (unlisted so students can't see them in advance by accident).

7. Create a QR code for each clue video.

8. Create a sheet for each group to fill out as they go along.

9. Place the QR codes in the locations for the hunt.

10. Divide the students up in groups of three to four and send them out for the hunt.

Bonus: For added engagement, have the students record their own video responses to each clue.

Scavenger hunts have been around forever. Most kids have done them before, so they can get stale quickly. So why not up the wow factor by adding video elements to your scavenger hunts?

Imagine instead of finding clues to the next item or location, students find a QR code taped to the wall with a note that says "Play Me." No other instructions. When they watch the video, a "guest" tells them the tale of that day's quest. As they go through the hunt, each new video moves the story along and introduces them to new perils and new rewards. This approach takes something old and makes it new again—one of my specialties.

Themes are the key to making this a success. The type of theme isn't important. It's all about tying everything together. I've seen some extraordinary themes centered on space exploration, time travel to ancient lands, an epic journey to the center of the earth, and scientists trying to solve a murder. The goal is to have everything connected to one central idea.

Scavenger hunts can deliver content, but students also work on communication with group members, time management, leadership, and other group dynamics that are essential for work beyond school.

Most important, these treks make learning fun!

Video EDITS

POSSIBLE APPLICATIONS: Teacher to Student

Several years ago, you would find me on a typical Friday leaving school with my arms straining as I carried two giant tubs of papers and spiral notebooks, a messenger bag slung over my shoulder, and a coffee thermos dangling precariously between two fingers, praying I wouldn't drop anything. I rarely thought ahead, so of course my car door would be locked. Then I would balance a hundred pounds of student learning on one knee while I shuffled through the items in my pocket—school ID, headphones, cell phone, finally keys. On a good day, I'd get the door unlocked and drop the bundle into the front seat. Just as likely, I would drop one or more items and run around the nearly deserted parking lot chasing loose essays. I can't tell you how many times I had to apologize for dirt or tire marks on a returned paper. (There were also a few times I had to apologize for donut crumbs on their papers, but we won't get into that.) Once all materials were accounted for and the door was shut, I would trudge back into the building for my second load.

Thanks to the use of technology, including online grading, I now carry home a lot less work. I've also

STUDENT-CREATED VIDEO

Peer conferencing is a great way for students to get feedback on their writing quickly, and it helps them clean up their drafts before I see them, but sometimes it can be intimidating for a student to make comments and suggestions to a classmate. So instead, have students record their feedback on video. Students probably don't want their writing feedback posted online, so have the students record directly on their classmate's device or AirDrop the videos. Before students get started, be sure to give them examples of constructive peer feedback and a live demonstration on the big screen.

VIDEO FEEDBACK SCREENCASTS

Ingredients:

tripod (optional)

microphone (optional)

screencast program

student writing

Awesome Sauce

Prep Time: 2 to 3 minutes

Recording Time: 3 to 7 minutes

Directions:

1. (Optional) Have the students email you asking for video feedback. (This makes step 9 much easier.)

2. Open the student's writing document and your screencasting program. If it is a handwritten assignment, then just open up the camera on your recording device.

3. Connect your microphone if you are using one.

4. Read through the writing one time without recording. (Sometimes I record on the fly without reading the student's work ahead of time, but it takes a lot of practice and knowledge of each student's common writing errors to do this right).

5. Start recording.

6. (Optional) Read the essay out loud.

7. Point out a couple of strengths and a couple of areas for improvement. Highlight on the screen while you are commenting.

8. End the recording.

9. E-mail the feedback video to the students, AirDrop the video (if the device allows you to), or post the video on YouTube unlisted and send the link.

Check out this example: youtu.be/ITsMu144Xuk

streamlined the art of giving helpful, timely feedback on student writing. In the past I would read an essay, spend five to seven minutes poring over every detail, scribble notes all over the page, and hand it back. Students would then read every suggestion in rapt silence. They would go back to their essays and produce amazing scholarly works. Not only would they make all of my suggested changes, they would then come up and personally thank me for improving their work. They would praise me for my teaching prowess, and then clean up their desk and floor area on their way out the door. In the hall I would overhear them discussing the invigorating lesson they had just experienced and discuss how lucky they were to have a teacher so dedicated to take the time to give such awe-inspiring feedback. They would adorn my door with banners in honor of my awesomeness and...

Okay, maybe that was a dream I had once. I usually found their essays in the recycling bin. (I'm sure they took a picture of it and were going to make their corrections at home.)

Feedback is only helpful if it is meaningful to students. Written feedback often looks like a roadmap of all the ways the student has failed. I needed something that would engage the students while still giving me time to give feedback. That's when I found that video edits were feedback gold.

For each major writing assignment, I record a quick video outlining what corrections need to be made. I usually focus on a couple of main points to help students improve their writing. Sometimes these videos consist of a screencast of me walking a student through their essay. Other times they might show me reading through the writing and giving feedback that way.

The feedback depends on the students. Some students respond better when they can see my face while I'm talking to them. (A lot of times these are the same students who can't watch me live for five minutes without getting off track. Maybe I'm more photogenic on the small screen?)

I give video feedback on any assignment students would like feedback on. If a student is willing to take the time to ask, I'm more than happy to carve out a couple minutes to help them out. They e-mail their essay to me and I send them video feedback. I love a good face-to-face conference and meet with the students whenever I can, but this is a great fill-in between meetings.

SPELLING *Review*

POSSIBLE APPLICATIONS: Teacher to Student

I remember getting a spelling booklet in fifth grade. It was the same type of spelling booklet I had received for the previous three years: it had fill-in-the-blanks, spaces to write sentences, and matching activities for all my spelling words. Everyone received the same list. For each list of words, you took a pretest on Monday and a posttest on Friday. I thought it was stupid, so I didn't do it. And of course, I got in trouble for not completing my work. About a month into school I found out that one of my friends liked to do spelling packets, so I had him do mine, too. I always did great on the spelling tests, because

STUDENT-CREATED VIDEO

Teaching something to someone else can have a profound impact on a student's ability to recall information. What better way to practice spelling words than to create spelling review videos? These can be done a couple of different ways:

1. Students work in groups to record a video of all of the words.

2. Each student gets a different word and records an interesting video to help classmates remember how the word is spelled.

3. Students work in pairs and divide the list in half. Each student records a video of words for their partner. They combine their words at the end.

Whichever way you divide the videos up, create a master playlist of all of the videos for the students to study from. As an added bonus, you can compile a GIANT playlist and mix older words into every spelling test to increase recall.

the words I was given were easy for me and the packets never added to my knowledge base.

I admit, I probably could have handled the situation better. Spelling packets didn't cut it then, and they don't cut it now. Spice it up. I teach middle school and don't have spelling lists. My wife, Jenica Stock, a fifth-grade teacher at Washington Elementary School, does. She does everything she can to make sure those words come alive for her students, including making spelling videos that go along with her spelling lists.

First, she records general videos of her spelling lists: these are simple videos of her reading each spelling word. (She has different lists for different ability levels.) These videos can be combined with various activities; they're a way for students to quiz themselves over the words along with the teacher, even when she can't be

right there with them. They can pause the video and write the word without having to stress out that the next word is coming up or everyone is waiting for them to finish.

She then creates different activity videos for independent practice. These might include sentences with the words in them, actions to help remember the words, or instructions on how to complete a word game at their desks. These videos give the students control over their learning and the independence to perform the tasks on their own. It also gives them choice in how they want to learn the words.

Finally, my wife creates spelling test videos. Students follow along with these videos to take their test.

SPELLING REVIEW ACTIVITY

Ingredients:

recording device (I usually just use my phone)

tripod (optional)

spelling list

Awesome Sauce

Prep Time: 5 to 10 minutes

Recording Time: 5 to 10 minutes

Difficulty: ● ○ ○ ○ ○

Check out this example: youtu.be/5ZEvBgDi2sY

Directions:

1. Decide on a theme for your words. (For example, if you choose words with a spooky twist to them, you could create a spooky video theme.)

2. Decide on a setting for your video. (For example, a dark room with a flashlight shining on your face.)

3. Record the spelling words for students to practice. Pause after each word to give the students time to write them down. At various points in the video, remind the students to pause the video if they need more time.

4. Post the video on YouTube.

5. Share the video with students.

A video of her reading words sounds boring, and it would be if that were all she did. But instead of sticking with the repetitive boring videos, she spices them up and adds a heaping spoonful of Awesome Sauce. She brings in guests (I've been known to make an appearance from time to time), records in unique locations, and sometimes throws out challenges in the middle of her videos.

Since all the fifth-grade classes use the same spelling lists, teachers are able to divide and conquer. Sharing the workload gives them the opportunity to enjoy a library of great video resources.

Gamification

POSSIBLE APPLICATIONS: Teacher to Student

Dr. Vonn Stock is my archnemesis. As far as my students are concerned, he is my evil twin brother who relishes the chance to make my life miserable, whether it's sending his henchmen after me or leaving rude notes on my board. (Lately he's even taken to writing recruitment notes on random pages in my students' notebooks.) His favorite thing to do is interrupt the daily announcements to share some evil message or to mock me.

STUDENT-CREATED VIDEO

Side quests are a huge part of my gamified class. A side quest is a challenge activity where students take a deeper dive into the content. Most of the side quests in my game require students to share what they have learned in an interesting way. Often this involves recording videos. In the past students have done things like the following:

1. Record a reenactment of a story they wrote.

2. Record a screencast of a Minecraft world they created based on the setting of the book they were reading.

3. Record a public service announcement using persuasive techniques we studied in class.

4. Record a video explaining how star navigation works and share it with their science class.

Some days students walk into a video update of Dr. V.'s evilness, or they'll watch video updates from my assistants, the valiant (although fairly stupid) Special Agents A–Z, who are trying to help me defeat the big evil baddie in my classroom game, A Novel Quest.

A Novel Quest started a couple years ago when I had an idea: What if I transformed my classroom from the traditional model where students sit at desks while I funneled content into their minds? What if I did something that would engage my students and make them excited to come to school each day? I've always loved games, ever since I was a little kid. My family always played board games, card games, video games, and so on. What if I brought some of those game elements into my classroom?

I decided to add as many different game mechanics to my class as possible, including things like dice battles, boss battles, and chance cards. All of this is designed to get the kids competing to "level up" and move up on the online

GAME INSTRUCTION MANUAL

Ingredients:

recording device (I usually just use my phone)

tripod (optional)

list of game rules (you can add to this throughout the year, so start with the basics)

pictures of items from the game

Awesome Sauce

Prep Time: 10 to 15 minutes

Recording Time: 15 to 30 minutes

Difficulty: ● ● ● ● ○

Check out this example: youtu.be/xLlvdmGQPJc

Directions:

1. Make a list of all of the current rules for your gamified class.

2. Make a list of any items students can collect in your gamified class. These could be things like an amulet that lets them sit in a sacred seat in the room or a sword that helps them battle a villain in your game.

3. Make a list of chance cards for your gamified class. These could be things like a treasure chest card that gives the student bonus points or a card that lets the student move to the front of a line. My favorite in my class is the Robin Hood card that lets a team steal points from one team, but they have to give it to another team.

4. Include a section for leaderboards, badges, and prizes.

5. Record a separate video explaining each section above.

6. Add some epic gaming music to each video.

7. For extra Awesome Sauce, add video game sound effects.

8. Upload each video to YouTube.

9. Create a playlist of game instruction videos on YouTube.

10. Share the playlist with students.

points leaderboard by learning my content. (A lot of my ideas come from the book *Explore Like a Pirate* by Michael Matera.)

Have you ever watched a kid play video games? They'll spend four hours playing the exact same level, lose 200 times, and still pick up the controller to try again. To bring my students that kind of excitement, I made my class into its own video/board game.

My videos are used to push the story forward and move students to the next level. They add texture and variation, break up the monotony, and make the content seem new and exciting.

The best part is that the students don't realize that while they are engaging in various game mechanics, they are also diving deep into content. They are getting a thorough understanding of curricular concepts and at the same time working on communication skills, collaboration, time management, organization, being a good sport, and much, much more.

SCREENCASTING *Writing*

POSSIBLE APPLICATIONS: Teacher to Student

Writing is hard. For everyone. I'm sitting here writing this book and I keep reflecting on that fact. It gets easier over time as you add more tools in your writing toolbox, but every writer will tell you the same thing.

Students have just as much trouble, if not more. They struggle with writing, and they don't yet have many tools for great writing in their arsenal. They may not even know what tools they need. Our job as teachers is to show them the tools that craft good writing...and maybe share with them a little of the Awesome Sauce that makes good writing great.

I want students to see me struggle through a piece of writing. They build up this image in their minds that great writers sit down at the computer and the words pour out in a perfect draft that will engage readers, that great writers don't even need backspace or delete buttons because their writing is so phenomenal.

I don't want to just show students something I've written; I want them to see and hear me struggle through my first draft. The best way to do that is to actually write in front of them. This is terrifying. It's one of the hardest things I've done in the classroom, because it makes you as vulnerable as the kids. But they love it. They love to see that you struggle, too.

I show them the truth multiple times throughout the year by doing screencasts of myself writing an essay. The first time I do this—usually the first time I introduce persuasive writing—I let them choose the topic for me. We brainstorm a set of topics, and then we vote on the best one. They vote which side of the argument I'm supposed to champion. Then I record. And sometimes it is brutal.

To screencast this, I put my writing up on the big screen and hit record on my screencasting program. Then I start typing and talking through my text. I'm very transparent. If I don't like something, I'll say, "That didn't sound quite right,"

SCREENCASTING WRITING

Ingredients:

computer

microphone

screencasting program

Awesome Sauce

Prep Time: 2 to 5 minutes

Recording Time: 7 to 10 minutes

Difficulty: ● ● ● ● ●

Directions:

1. Plug in the microphone if it isn't built in.
2. Open the screencasting program.
3. Open a fresh document to write in.
4. Push record and start writing.
5. Talk as you type out your responses.
   - Point out times when you are confused.
   - Explain why you delete certain things.
   - Explain why you aren't happy with something and that you want to come back to it later.
6. Stop recording.
7. Share the video and the finished document with the students.
8. Repeat with any other classes but try to use a different topic each time. This keeps things fresh.

Check out this example: youtu.be/YM7x_q6kQyE

or, "That didn't make sense." Sometimes I'll be blunt and say, "That was stupid." I talk through my entire inner monologue. It's raw and uncut. When I'm done recording, I post the video on Google Classroom for students to refer back to later when they are doing their own writing. Usually by the end of the recording I have a decent draft that they can use as a model when they start writing.

Other times I'll do the screencast at home and post it with a new assignment. The best example happened last summer. A major flaw in my building is that only seven or eight classrooms in the entire school have windows. Due to the school's age and numerous additions, most of the classrooms are on inside walls that don't ever get sunlight. Last summer, after spending ten years in a dungeon, never seeing the light of day, I learned that a classroom with giant windows had opened up. And I wanted it!

At first, I wrote a generic email asking the principal if I could switch class-rooms. The next day, I thought about it, and I realized that another opportunity like this might not come along for a long time. I didn't want to miss this chance. I needed something that would help me stand out. What could I possibly do? I brought the focus back to the students.

I recorded a screencast walking through a persuasive letter explaining why I wanted that classroom. I went through the entire process, from brainstorming ideas to writing out the draft to editing it. I talked about some reasons I liked but that weren't quite strong enough arguments. I talked to the students about writing purpose and etiquette. Because my letter was a more formal request, I told the students that even though I'm on a first-name basis with the principal, I would address him as "Mr. Libal." I talked about how some reasons sounded ruder than I wanted, so I deleted those.

When I was finished, I sent the screencast, the letter, and an explanation to my principal. It turned out to be a phenomenal real-world experience for the kids to witness. I knew it would be a great model for the positive outcomes of persuasive writing.

And then I got the e-mail that said I wouldn't be getting that room.

I'm kidding. I spent the rest of the summer moving my furniture into my new room with a view.

5

The Main Course
(Part II: Differentiation)

Each year, educators are challenged to deliver content to students at a wide range of ability levels. These videos provide different ways to differentiate for all learners.

IN-CLASS *Flipping*

POSSIBLE APPLICATIONS: Teacher to Student

Flipped learning is flipping awesome—in theory.

If you're not familiar with the concept, flipped learning involves flipping the direct instruction or first learning opportunity of a topic from a whole-class lecture model to an independent learning model: students are guided through the learning on their own outside of class, then have the opportunity to practice that learning in the classroom with the guidance of their teacher.

I love this idea of having a teacher there to guide students through the application portion of the learning process. Students need the opportunity to explore content at their own pace. They need powerful tools to allow them to rewatch, relearn, and sometimes even speed through content at the pace that helps them learn best. They need the chance to experience a wide range of content and explore new things. Flipping the classroom can do all of that—again, in theory.

My struggle with the flipped classroom is that homework is still homework. The kids who didn't do their essay at home are the same ones who won't watch my flipped videos, no matter how engaging they are. I'll also be honest: some things in every content area are boring but important to learn about. I can create engaging lessons, interesting videos, and captivating ideas, but some ideas will never appeal to everyone.

The issue of equity also comes up. I teach in a Title I school where about 25% of students don't have reliable access to the internet at home. Their parents may have cell phones with internet access but not enough data to let the students watch a large number of videos. They may have access to free Wi-Fi at hot spots around the city, but expecting a kid to hang out at a coffee shop three nights a week to work on homework is problematic. I know some incredible educators who work hard to make this work: for instance, offering iPods with the videos uploaded on them or burning DVDs. All of that is amazing, but not a practical long-term solution.

So as great as the flipped learning model sounds, roadblocks often derail some awesome flipping ideas. If you are one of those remarkable teachers who find a

FLIPPING AWESOME IN-CLASS FLIPPED VIDEOS

Ingredients:

recording device (I usually just use my phone)

tripod (optional)

screencasting tool

lesson plan

lesson materials

Prep Time: 10 to 15 minutes

Recording Time: 15 to 30 minutes

Difficulty: ● ● ● ● ●

Directions:

1. Plan out the details of the lesson.
2. Create a slideshow of your lesson.
3. Record a screencast of the slideshow; add video of you as you present in the corner of the presentation if possible
4. Post the video on YouTube.
5. Share the video with students.

Check out this example: youtu.be/m_yeReOT0b4

way to get students engaged in flipped learning, you are a rock star and should continue doing what you are doing. If not, consider the "in-class flip" model.

I first heard about the in-class flip model from Jennifer Gonzalez's *Cult of Pedagogy* podcast. (If you haven't listened to that podcast, I highly recommend it!) She also describes the technique in an article for *Edutopia* (Gonzalez, 2014). This model takes advantage of the best pieces of the flipped model (guiding students through content with video lessons), but instead of watching the videos at home, students watch the videos in class. They can pause the videos, rewind, and rewatch if they get confused. Students who are rocking the content can move ahead more quickly, and students who are struggling can move at a slower pace.

The best part of the in-class flip model is that it frees me up to work with individual students or small groups. While students are working through the videos, I can walk around the room, gauge attention and focus, and step in with students who might need additional support. Furthermore, for the kids who finish early, I can expand on the lesson with challenges that help develop a deeper understanding of a topic. Few things frustrate me more than seeing a student who is brilliant in a content area finish early, then either be given more of the same work or be told to figure out something else to work on. I want to push and guide those students just as much as the students who are struggling.

The next three sections are all ways to use the in-class flip model to differentiate student learning, especially the pacing of lessons. (This is just a general recipe structure; more details are included in the next sections.)

TEST *Review*

POSSIBLE APPLICATIONS: Teacher to Student

I don't use tests to assess my students very often. I try to get a wide range of data points to assess what a student knows, using approaches such as in-class observations, some sort of activity involving collaboration and problem solving, and assorted written responses. However, when I do have a test or quiz (which I call "skills checks"), I love to use videos to prep the students.

The process usually starts several days before a test. I'll share a video with students, either as a whole class or during a rotation to help them complete an assignment. The videos allow me to add real-world connections to what we are studying and give visual cues to help students recall the information we are working with.

All through high school, college, and into my teaching career, I waited tables at a pizza place. (Someday I'll pay off those student loans.) There were a lot of late nights finishing up in the restaurant with a stack of essays to grade sitting on a back counter. One night after work, I decided to record a video in the restaurant talking about my night. Throughout the night, I worked on coming up with different ideas to study for a skills check on similes and metaphors. It was a busy night, and we had quite a few interesting people to talk about. I shared the true tale of a group of kids whose parents didn't bother to watch them. The kids, whom I referred to as Oompa Loompa monsters, managed to crush crackers under the table for most of the night. I also described what it was like bouncing around the restaurant like a bouncy ball.

In the video, I also took the students on a tour of the restaurant. I showed them what it looks like at night when there aren't any customers, and I took them on a tour of the kitchen. It was a behind-the-scenes look at something they might otherwise not get to see, so I thought it might add a little fun to the video. The guys in the kitchen thought it was hilarious and asked to watch my video when I was done.

The next day I brought in the video and played it for the students. They loved hearing the stories about the people I waited on, and they really enjoyed seeing the back of the restaurant, which they don't normally get to see. After I played the video, I had the students get out a piece of paper and make a T-chart on the page. They labeled one column "simile" and the other "metaphor." Then I challenged them to write down all of the examples of similes and metaphors as I played the video again. They competed to see who could catch the most and label them correctly.

The video brought something different: it was looking at something we had talked about for weeks, but in a new way. The competition also helped with this.

Another video I created was for a review of prefixes and suffixes. This was early in my teaching career. I knew my students were especially struggling with suffixes. I decided the best tool for this would be action figures (obviously).

I wrote a script at school for a series of videos, one for each prefix and suffix. When I arrived home, I told my wife I was going to be working for school. Thirty minutes later, she came into the kitchen to find me lying on the floor playing with Buzz Lightyear and Batman action figures. I believe at the exact moment she came in I was crashing a tiny car into the action figures and making explosion sounds. I think at that point she was questioning my "work."

The video turned out fantastic. I added the videos to a PowerPoint presentation with the prefix or suffix at the top of each slide. This combination of text and video was a great test review. Not only could students watch it during class, they were also able to watch it at home while they studied for the test.

Providing students with video reviews along with traditional study guides and in-class activities gives students multiple entry points into the content. They can choose the method that works best.

STUDENT—CREATED VIDEO

Older kids love an excuse to play with their childhood toys. I love to find ways to encourage them to use those to demonstrate concepts. To review for an upcoming assessment, have students bring in old toys from home. I always keep a backup set at school for kids who forget to bring them. Then give them the concepts you want them to review. Have them record a video demonstrating the concept. Then share those with the students as a part of their study materials.

TEST REVIEWS

Ingredients:

recording device (I usually just use my phone)

tripod (optional)

topic to review

script (optional)

interesting setting

Awesome Sauce

Prep Time: 10 to 15 minutes

Recording Time: 5 to 15 minutes

Difficulty: ● ● ● ● ●

Directions:

1. Plan out the purpose of the video. What content are you trying to work on?

2. Look for the best spot to record the video. Think about things like background noise.

3. Read through the script.

4. Record the video. Focus on only one or two concepts. If there are more concepts to cover, consider doing a series of four- to six-minute videos.

5. Post the video(s) on YouTube.

6. Share the video(s) with students.

Check out this example: youtu.be/ZAgnzUEB4r8

Guided READING

POSSIBLE APPLICATIONS: Teacher to Student

Every year, I get a new batch of students. Each year is different, but I always get a wide range of reading abilities. I usually have students who run the gamut from second- to twelfth-grade-level and everything in between. Keep in mind that my students are all sixth graders, so I have to find something for my students to read that will interest them at their current maturity level, but still find a way to match the reading to all ability levels. It's challenging. I allow for a lot of student choice in what they read. All year, they get to choose what interests them at varying reading levels. However, I see value in sometimes reading novels as a whole class.

This can be tricky. I try to find something that will keep my above-grade-level readers hooked but that is also manageable for my slightly below-grade-level students. The students who are reading two or more grade levels below are the main challenge. I strongly believe that a great book is a great book, and if I give students the right scaffolding, I can have all my students reading grade-level texts.

I *love* reading to/with my students. I love being there with them as they experience a story for the first time. I love talking to them about the parts that surprised them or angered them. I love that spark when they connect with a book.

But unless it's an extremely engaging novel, it's a challenge to study a text as a whole class. This is especially true for students who have executive functioning struggles. In a typical whole-class book study, some students may get lost during the reading process and never be able to catch up, while other students are bored.

Instead of doing a traditional whole-class reading of a novel, I record myself reading chapters of the books to the students.

I do this for a couple of reasons:

STUDENT-CREATED VIDEO

Story is a powerful thing. It's something that can have a profound impact on a child's inner reading voice. Most kids love being read to, especially by a strong reader who does voices and reads with emotion. Older students are great at reading to younger students, but sometimes schedules don't line up to make this work. Students can overcome this obstacle by recording videos of themselves reading their favorite children's books for younger students. They can share these videos in a variety of ways:

1. Send QR codes of the videos to be posted in elementary school libraries.

2. Create a playlist of the videos in YouTube and share the playlist with elementary school teachers.

3. Create bookmarks with QR codes on them and share them at the local public library.

4. Have students take their videos home to share with their siblings.

1. They can hear how a great reader reads. (I use the term "great" loosely. I think I'm a pretty great reader, but I'm definitely no Jim Dale, the amazing narrator of the U.S. *Harry Potter* audiobooks.) I want students to hear my attempts at reading different characters using different voices. They love it when I attempt a girl's voice or a child's voice. They love my terrible British accents. I also want them to hear how I speed up my reading at an intense moment or slow down during a calm part of the story. I want them to hear the way I sound out words I may not know and stumble over place names.

2. I can point out important parts of the text. I want them to home in on certain elements they may have missed. For most of our novels, this is my tenth-plus time reading it. I know which things connect to the themes of the novel and I point those out, although I try not to limit the conversation to my own observations. I always give students opportunities to share what they notice. I love it when they come up with something I've never thought of before.

3. I can show them what the inner dialogue of a great reader sounds like. I stop and ask students questions. I'll say things like, "I wonder why the author chose to single out that character?" or, "I can't figure out why she doesn't just run away." (By the way, the answers are because that character is a jerk and because she is a naive teen who doesn't know what adventures await her—both examples taken from *The True Confessions of Charlotte Doyle* by Avi). I'll make predictions that I made the first time I read the books. I'll talk about the characters I like and the ones I hate. Students love hearing what is going on in my head while I'm reading.

For the first half of the first novel we read, I require all my students to watch the videos while they follow along in the text. I do this because I want my readers who may struggle with the text to keep up with it, and my readers who are reading above grade-level to slow down. I find that a lot of my advanced readers want to race through the book and don't always take the time to reflect on what they're reading. It drives some of them crazy to slow down and stick with the video, but once they see how much fun I have in my readings, a lot of them stick with me through the whole novel.

About halfway through the novel, I give the students a choice: they can continue with the videos or read on their own. A lot of kids love reading with me and stick with the videos; a few want to read on their own and that's fine, too. Some students make a good choice. Others don't. I leave it to them to make that choice, but to help guide them to make a better one, I'll ask them a few questions about their current choice. If they can't answer the questions, I'll ask if they are making the best choice.

Some students need to be explicitly taught how to gauge their levels of both understanding and engagement in the reading. Students who struggle with reading comprehension may not realize when they aren't following a story. With the right prompting, students can learn to pause the video when they discover they

GUIDED READING POWERPOINT VIDEO

Ingredients:

recording device (I usually just use my phone)

tripod (optional)

text

guiding questions

Microsoft PowerPoint

Awesome Sauce

Prep Time: 10 to 15 minutes

Recording Time: 15 to 30 minutes (depending on the length of the text)

Difficulty: ● ● ● ● ○

Directions:

1. Select the text you want to record. Try to keep each recording to less than twenty minutes. If possible, break the chapter up into five- to six-minute chunks.

2. Create a PowerPoint slide with guiding questions for small sections of the text.

3. Record yourself reading the text using the built-in PowerPoint recording tools. Pause at the end of each section.

4. Tell the students to pause the video and record their responses somewhere, either with paper and pencil or a digital alternative.

5. Finalize the recording.

6. Post the video to YouTube.

7. Share the video with students.

Check out this example: youtu.be/d6h7CtVlX0w

Check out this example: youtu.be/zzovsGgn-_g

are not paying attention so that they can redirect and regroup. They can also learn to rewind the video and reread when they are confused.

The best part about using video for reading instruction is the freedom it gives me. I can devote the time and energy to teaching these skills to those students without slowing down other readers. Since I'm checking in with all of the students individually, they aren't singled out in front of the class. Every student is getting what they need when they need it.

I've been doing this for several years, and I've had great feedback not only from students, but also from parents. I had one mother tell me it was bizarre the first time she heard a strange voice coming from their kitchen. When she went to investigate, she saw her son sitting at the counter, book in hand, reading along with me. It was an especially intense part of our book, and she stood and watched the video with her son. Then she said she watched the rest of the videos. I laughed because I knew exactly which part she was talking about: One of the characters is dangling from the side of the mountain, so while I'm reading, my arms are flailing around while I'm acting out climbing up a mountain with ice axes in each hand. At one point, I even jump out of my chair, acting out a particularly intense paragraph. I may get a little carried away, but it engages my students.

Test ACCOMMODATIONS

POSSIBLE APPLICATIONS: Teacher to Student

Even though I give students as much choice as I possibly can in the ways they present their learning, some things are still best assessed with a quiz or test. I'm okay with those being a small dose of their yearly assessment diet; the trick is to make sure that the score is truly a measure of what the student knows, and that there's not some other factor getting in the way.

For example, if I'm assessing a writing skill, I don't want reading to get in the way. If the student is unfamiliar with a few words, I don't want those to derail the student's writing ability because they're confused about the meaning of a text. In the Guided Reading section I expressed the importance of accommodating different reading abilities in reading assignments. I make the same adjustments in the assessments I give to students. To help with this, I sometimes record videos of myself reading the texts. I don't give the videos to everyone, only to those whose Individualized Education Plans require accommodation.

> **STUDENT-CREATED VIDEO**
>
> Depending on the content, many assessments could be accommodated simply by allowing students to record a video responding to a prompt instead of writing out a response. To do this, add a QR code link on the assessment, directing students where to post their responses. Make sure to give them a quiet location to record.

Other times, some of my students need test questions read aloud. I've started including a video of me reading the questions on a QR code right on the test. Students who don't need questions read aloud get a different video

TEST ACCOMMODATIONS FOR STUDENTS WHO NEED ADDITIONAL SUPPORT

Ingredients:

recording device (I usually just use my phone)

tripod (optional)

test/quiz

QR code generator

Awesome Sauce

Prep Time: 3 to 5 minutes

Recording Time: 10 to 20 minutes, depending on the length of the test

Difficulty: ● ● ● ● ●

Directions:

1. Set up the recording device.
2. Get out a copy of the test. (Sometimes I may have three to four versions of a test, so I try to label the tests in some way.)
3. Begin recording.
4. Say which version of the test you are working with.
5. Give students a quick positive message reminding them that they are awesome and that you believe in them.
6. Read the test directions.
7. Read each test question and, if it's a multiple-choice test, all the possible answers.
8. Leave about three to five seconds between questions to give the students time to pause the video if they need more think time.
9. At the end of the video, ask them a reflection question. (I try to have this be one of the questions on the test, too.) Usually it's something like "How did you prepare for this test, and do you think you were ready for the test when you took it?"
10. Finish the recording.
11. Post the video on YouTube as an unlisted video.
12. Copy the video link into a QR code generator.
13. Copy the QR code onto the test or quiz.
14. Pass out the quiz to students and watch their awesomeness emerge.

Check out this example: youtu.be/nEPYSAJyjZU

reminding them to double-check their work. It's like I'm sitting right there cheering them on, and it reminds them that I'm not there to stump them. The test isn't a gotcha. It's just a check to see what they know.

Tests are supposed to be a form of communication between me and my students, letting both of us know what they've mastered and what they haven't mastered yet. I don't want outside factors influencing that.

PHYSICAL EDUCATION *Exercise* INSTRUCTIONS

POSSIBLE APPLICATIONS: Teacher to Student

I believe that video instructions can enhance any subject area. A quick video can say more than a diagram ever could. My best example of this is a series of exercise videos for physical education.

I gave up going to the gym a long time ago. One of the biggest reasons for this is because I felt stupid when I would walk in. Here's how my typical gym experience would go: First, I would enter the gym and do some stretches in a corner. I would try to think back to my middle school PE days. I'd stretch my arms and legs in what I'm assuming was good form. (At least it felt like I was stretching something; I assume it was muscle.) Then I would walk over to the treadmill. That machine I can do. I can walk or run in one spot. No problem. No big deal. That one isn't difficult. If that could work every muscle in my body, life would be good. Unfortunately, it can't.

STUDENT-CREATED VIDEO

After students have mastered a few workouts, challenge them to create their own plan, including videos to explain the workout. These could be a basic routine or a workout to prepare for a specific sport. They could even prepare a workout routine for a sport and then share it with younger kids. Take it to the next level by developing a plan to market their workout program.

When it was time to work my other muscles (is that what you call it? working other muscles?), I would walk around the machines like a lost four-year-old. I'd have a panicked look in my eyes and stare at these bizarre contraptions with bars and pins and metal. They looked like torture devices—and felt like them when I tried to use one. I'd look at the "friendly" diagrams on the wall. The diagrams made no sense whatsoever. I'm not even sure the diagram was for the machine I was looking at. Then I would attempt to repeat what I saw on the diagram. I'd try one or two times, feel stupid, and walk away.

WORKOUT TRAINING VIDEOS

Ingredients:

recording device (I usually just use my phone)

tripod (optional)

workout equipment

additional participants if needed

QR code generator

Awesome Sauce

Prep Time: 5 to 10 minutes

Recording Time: 10 to 30 minutes

Difficulty: ● ● ● ● ●

Directions:

1. Make a list of workouts students will be doing in the near future.

2. Set up the camera facing the workout equipment or workout space. Pay attention to things in the background and make sure you can get the entire workout in the shot.

3. Practice recording one or two times to make sure everything will be in the shot. (This is one video that would benefit from the use of a cameraperson.)

4. Begin recording the video. Have a participant perform the exercise while you point out the following:
   - safety
   - proper form for the workout
   - equipment needed
   - muscles worked (point to where the muscles are located)

5. Once the video is recorded, post it to YouTube.

6. Copy the video URL to a QR code generator website.

7. Post the QR code next to the workout equipment.

This is a QR code I have posted outside my room for kids who need a quick energy break during class.

 Check out this example: youtu.be/W5OkIzclU6g

Sometimes I would watch and wait until someone left a machine and just copy what they had done. You can only do that so many times before the person gets weirded out, and then you leave—quickly.

My point is, going to the gym is terrifying. And I'm a grown man who is not dealing with the challenges of adolescence. Working out is not only confusing to those of us who aren't physically inclined, it's also dangerous. If you work out incorrectly you can cause serious damage to your body. (This is one fact about the gym I know from personal experience. Intramural softball is no joke.)

A video tutorial of the different workouts could solve a lot of these issues. Just post a video illustrating how to do each workout using a QR code. That's it. That simple step could save students from getting hurt and/or looking stupid (which, in a middle schooler's mind, is probably worse than the physical pain).

A lot of elements in PE could benefit from this. Imagine you are doing a variety of stations around the gym. I know this is going to shock you, but sometimes when you're giving instructions, especially to a large group like a PE class, kids don't always pay attention. Just post a video reminder of each station, and your students will have no excuses for not doing the activity.

6

A La Carte:

A Little Bit of Everything

Some things simply don't fit into a specific category. The videos in this chapter provide different ways to engage students, teachers, and parents.

MEETING *Updates*

POSSIBLE APPLICATIONS: Teacher to Teacher, Administrator to Teacher, Administrator to Parent

I don't know if you are like me, but my e-mail is out of control. I'm sure you only get one or two e-mails a day, and they are the absolute most important things that get sent out. You probably never get e-mails that make you say things like, "Did they really just send that out?" or, "Do they actually teach, or just send e-mails all day?" My inbox is constantly bombarded with information about meetings, schedule changes, district-mandated items, "administrivia," messages from parents, and so much more. The barrage never ends. The worst ones are the e-mails that use multiple paragraphs to explain something that should only take a quick bulleted list.

In the past, our Building Leadership Team (BLT) sent out a detailed e-mail of our monthly meeting notes. We included everything we thought teachers would want to know more about. The e-mails were thorough in conveying the vision of BLT, but I think only a handful of teachers read through them; they just added to the clutter.

To help combat this problem, I started recording a quick two-minute video highlighting the main points from our meeting. I would record right after the meeting, so I wouldn't miss anything. It didn't take any time, and then I would send it out to the staff. Yes, this meant one more e-mail to teacher's inboxes, but the videos seemed to get more traction than the written messages. Teachers knew to expect these e-mail videos and could quickly get all the information they needed from them.

I received a lot of positive feedback from staff on these messages. They liked the format because they could watch the video while doing other tasks. It highlighted the main points and made life simpler for them. They also liked being addressed directly by someone from the committee.

STUDENT-CREATED VIDEO

School staff strive to make informed decisions, and some of the best decisions we've made at my school have included student feedback. When it's not possible to bring students in to give their feedback during a meeting, an alternative is to record video input from students explaining their views on new initiatives, then share it at the beginning of a discussion of that initiative. This brings the focus back to the students and what they need most.

MEETING SUMMARY VIDEOS

Ingredients:

recording device (I usually just use my phone)

tripod (optional)

Awesome Sauce

Prep Time: 2 to 5 minutes

Recording Time: 2 to 5 minutes

Difficulty: ● ● ● ● ●

Directions:

1. Write down a list of the five to ten most important things that happened at the meeting.

2. Narrow that list down to three or four items.

3. Record a video naming the committee hosting the meeting, the date of the meeting, and the three or four items.

4. Make sure to wrap up with some sort of positive takeaway from the meeting along with any action steps staff members may need to take.

5. Post the video on YouTube. You can post it as an unlisted video if you don't want this to be a widely shared video.

6. Share the video with staff.

Check out an example: youtu.be/skZjW5Nv328

I still included the detailed notes for teachers who wanted to comb through everything. The video just added another option for teachers to get their information. Teachers are like students; they want choice in their lives. They want to be able to choose the method for getting information that works best for them.

Videos are a great way to cut down the amount of information presented at school faculty meetings. We've all sat in those meetings where, just when you think it's over, someone stands up and begins a "quick" spiel on the intricacies of proper supply-ordering protocol, or the step-by-step procedure for filling out a discipline referral. (As I'm describing this, you're probably thinking about that one person right now. We all have one.)

Instead of taking away from the time teachers get to spend with their families, do them a favor and flip that meeting. Send out a video updating all of the administrivia stuff that doesn't require a face-to-face discussion. A lot of that stuff is important, and teachers will appreciate the info much more when they can watch it from the comfort of their homes. Not only does the video shorten the faculty meeting, it also makes it easier to streamline what you want to say. You get a couple of takes if you need it, so you can highlight the essentials.

Staff will thank you for the Awesome Sauce!

Substitute PLANS

POSSIBLE APPLICATIONS: Teacher to Student

Plans for Students

I have had some fantastic substitute teachers, people who interact with students and accomplish everything I want them to accomplish. They engage the students in conversation and push the kids just as much as I would have. It's the next best thing to my being with the kids.

The problem is that I'm *not* with the kids. Sometimes my instructions to the substitute aren't clear enough, and sometimes the students need more explanations than the substitute can offer. Other times the class goes off on a tangent I never intended, and the pacing of the class gets disrupted.

One of the best ways to avoid any confusion is to include videos with your sub plans. My substitute prep usually goes something like this:

First, I pray that my students are going to be the respectful, helpful kids I know they can be. I have some astounding students, but they're still middle schoolers who sometimes have off days like anyone else. (For the record, 99% of the time it goes great.)

Next, I consider what I would do if I were at school that day. The beauty of language arts class is that it's easy for me to connect just about any text to what we've been working on lately, but I try not to stray too far from our current classroom trajectory.

I look at what instructions I need to deliver for the students to achieve the desired outcomes for the day. I may scale down expectations since I won't be there. Then I look at how I can add video instructions to help give all the directions the students need for the day.

I'm fortunate to teach in a school with 1:1 iPads, so I usually post the videos on Google Classroom for students to watch at the beginning of class. Each video starts the same way: "You have a substitute today. They are a guest in our room, and you should be helpful, courteous, and amazing representatives of this school. You are awesome. Make sure they know that."

Along with the announcement video, I usually include an outline of the day, as well as any other videos or documents students may need. Then they are ready to get started. A lot of my class is self-paced, so students are already used to working independently. The videos give instructions for things that may be new.

The substitute's role is to engage with the students and keep them on track. The notes from the substitutes in my room have been great. They love that the video clears things up, and they love that the self-paced element cuts down on behavior issues. The goal is for everyone to have a clear understanding of classroom expectations and their role in having an awesome day.

Plans for the Substitute

Imagine walking into a classroom for the first time. You don't know the school or the students well. You may not be comfortable with the curriculum, and you have to learn an entire lesson fifteen minutes before you deliver it. On top of that, you have a five-page document with notes on everything you need to attempt to accomplish that day. Or you have a two-sentence explanation jotted down on the back of on old worksheet that you had to crawl under the desk to pick up because it somehow fell off.

I can't imagine how challenging it is to be a substitute. My wife did it for a year and had a random grab bag of experiences ranging from remarkably detailed plans to what-am-I-supposed-to-do-with-this, I-guess-we're-going-to-have-to-wing-it-today plans. It's a rough job, and I'm extremely grateful for the people who tackle it each day.

My goal this year is to make it as easy as possible for them, and as I was typing up this chapter, I had an epiphany: What if I recorded an explanation video for the substitutes who come into my room, explaining everything they need to know for the day? I'll still include written instructions, but sometimes you can say more in a short amount of time in a video than you can with a page of notes.

That is my mission this school year. I'm sure it will be a whole batch of Awesome Sauce.

SUBSTITUTE WELCOME VIDEOS

Ingredients:

recording device (I usually just use my phone)

tripod (optional)

lesson plans for the day

Awesome Sauce

Prep Time: 5 to 10 minutes

Recording Time: 5 to 10 minutes

Difficulty: ● ● ● ● ●

Directions:

1. Create the lesson plans for the day, including printed copies of any documents students will be working with.

2. Record an introduction to your class, including a little bit about your students (particularly those who might be extra helpful). Also mention teachers who can answer questions and any out-of-the-ordinary events that might occur that day, such as students leaving for a field trip or a fire drill.

3. Walk through step-by-step instructions for each part of the lessons for the day.

4. Hold up any paper documents that students will be working with, so the substitute can see exactly what the students need to work on.

5. Wrap up the video with a thank you plus any last-minute tips. (For example, I usually offer substitutes bottled water and soda that I have in my fridge.)

6. Post the video unlisted on YouTube or post it in another location that can be easily shared.

7. Create a QR code of the video.

8. Attach a link to the video and the QR code to the sub plans.

Check out this example: youtu.be/9grQKtogU6o

TECHNOLOGY *Walkthroughs*

"Use four wood planks. No, the other wood planks. That's a block. Do you want me to do it?" the student asked in frustration.

He was trying to teach me how to make a crafting table in Minecraft. I didn't know how to make a crafting table, and I also wasn't quite sure what a crafting table was and why I needed one in the first place. (In all honesty, I just had to Google how to make it again, because I couldn't remember what this student had showed me.)

The point is, technology is tough for everyone. I'm a self-proclaimed tech geek, but I don't begin to come near the levels of geekdom of some of my more tech-savvy friends. And if you ask any one of them if they ever get frustrated or confused with technology, 100% of them will say yes.

We make assumptions about students. Since many of them have grown up with technology, we assume that it comes easy to them. This isn't always the case. They are not the "digital natives" people assume they are. Sure, they're tech-savvy with the technology they use all the time; they probably know the ins and outs of YouTube or Instagram. But ask them where the Shift key is on the keyboard, and a lot of them will give you a blank stare. Many of them also struggle with what to do when something goes wrong.

That is why I try to make technology walkthroughs for my students. I make them for the basic features of the majority of apps and websites we use frequently. I create videos for the following:

- turning in an assignment on Google Classroom

- accessing the textbook website

- checking grades online

- creating a new document

- connecting to the district Wi-Fi

- accessing e-mail

- sending an e-mail

- checking Google Classroom

- adding an event to their calendar

- setting an alarm on their calendar

- using online storage

- the inner workings of various content-specific apps

I also teach students how to find answers to new problems as they come up, because problems always will come up. That's the funny thing about technology: as helpful as it is, it

STUDENT-CREATED VIDEO

Several years ago, when Instagram first came out, I didn't understand it. I knew how to use Twitter and Facebook, but Instagram was new to me. I had a couple of former students show me how to set it up. Imagine if you had students demonstrate how to use apps in the classroom. Work with the students on recording screencasts for new technology, then share the recordings with staff members. This is especially helpful if it is an app that students love to use. Staff members will find it useful, and it will make students invested in making sure the technology works. For example, a few years ago I had students put together videos showcasing ways to use Minecraft in different subject areas. I told them that the more convincing the videos were and the better they connected to content, the more likely it would be that teachers would actually let them use it.

TECHNOLOGY TUTORIALS

Ingredients:

screencasting program

microphone

list of features of the tool

Awesome Sauce

Prep Time: 10 to 15

Recording Time: 10 to 15 minutes

Level of difficulty: ● ● ● ● ●

Directions:

1. Make a list of no more than five things you want to show the students. (If you have more to show, create multiple videos.)
2. Open the screencasting program on the device.
3. Open the program you want to do a tutorial for.
4. Push record.
5. If this is the first tutorial for this program, app, or tech feature, make sure to start by showing how to open it.
6. Walk through the list of features that you want to point out.
7. Finish recording.
8. Post your video on YouTube.
9. Share the video with students through a website or some other means such as Google Classroom.

Check out this example: youtu.be/GiNaYgtATus

always finds a way to stop working at the worst possible time. Students need to know how to use things like YouTube and Google to troubleshoot any technology problems. (Teachers could probably use the same training.)

I also make sure these technology videos are available to parents. As a parent myself, I can say firsthand that it is really frustrating trying to help my daughter fix or access something for her homework if I have absolutely no idea what the program is for. As a teacher, I try to cover all the basics, because I remember how confused I was the first time I used that technology.

7

Dessert:
The Sweetness That Makes It Great

The beauty of video is the way it can enhance any lesson. These videos provide different ways to spice up an existing lesson or add a layer of frosting to new content. They also pair well with many of the other videos included in this book.

STOP-MOTION *Videos*

POSSIBLE APPLICATIONS: Teacher to Student

For decades, people have been stringing together still images to make a movie. Whether it's Gumby, *Rudolph the Red-Nosed Reindeer,* or more recently *Coraline* or *Kubo and the Two Strings,* stop-motion animation has been entertaining audiences for decades. The realism mixed with fantasy makes it an ideal medium for transporting the audience into the world of the story.

Today, technology has advanced to a point where it's as easy to put together stop-motion videos as it is to take a photo. The process usually involves taking a series of photos in an app, then watching as the app magically strings them together. It's easy to add special effects, sound effects, and a music score to make an exciting film in mere minutes.

Sometimes it's easy to get stuck in a rut. When students see the exact same presentation style over and over and over (even Awesome Sauce videos), they start to tune out the content. It's like driving the same way to work every day: eventually you don't notice what's going on around you. Adding an element like stop-motion video keeps students engaged.

I like to pair stop-motion with my other video techniques to add a unique twist. For example, I love creating stop-motion videos for my announcements. Telling the students that they have a reading assignment due on Friday is one thing; it's quite another when Superman flies into the screen and a speech bubble appears above his head announcing the same assignment while Wonder Woman and the Flash do silly dances in the background.

I've also used stop-motion for reteaching lessons. I'll write out text and have characters act out a scene. I can easily emphasize important parts of my lesson by having characters dance around the text. If I tried to do this all the time, it would get tiresome, and it would be too much for me to keep up with. In short spurts, however, it's the perfect change of pace.

These videos can be done a couple of different ways. Sometimes I'll use characters cut out of construction paper with magnets stuck to the back. These are great, because I can stick them to my whiteboard and move them around easily. I can also write word bubbles and thought bubbles on the board to add dialogue and make my point.

MAGNETIC STOP—MOTION ANIMATION

Ingredients:

recording device (I usually just use my phone)

tripod

printed-out character pictures

magnets

magnetic dry-erase board

dry-erase markers

painter's tape

Awesome Sauce

Prep Time: 10 to 15 minutes (first time, can be reused after that)

Recording Time: 30-plus minutes

Level of difficulty: ● ● ● ● ●

Directions:

1. Cut out pictures of characters you want to animate.

2. Laminate the pictures (optional).

3. Glue magnets to the back of the characters.

4. Stick the characters on a magnetic dry-erase board.

5. Set up the recording device on the tripod facing the dry-erase board.

6. Look through the screen and use the painter's tape to tape the outer edge of the frame (make sure you can't see the tape in the screen). This helps you know where to put the characters so they are still in the shot.

7. Plan out a script of what you want to include in the video.

8. Take three to five pictures of the first image you want in your video in the stop-motion app of your choice.

9. Move the characters slightly (one to two inches) and take another picture.

10. Continue moving characters slightly in the directions you want them to go and take a picture after each move.

11. If you add text, thought bubbles, or speech bubbles, first draw the bubble and take a picture. Then add the text one letter at a time, taking a picture after each letter.

12. Continue this process slowly until you have taken all the pictures.

13. Some apps will let you add music and other special features.

14. **Optional:** You can upload the video to video-editing software and add more special effects to the video.

15. Once the video is complete, upload it to YouTube.

16. Share the video with your students.

Check out this example: youtu.be/dHuRPAnZ5h0

Other times I'll take out my bucket of toys—I mean, collectibles. I'll set up a few of them, then, using a little patience and tape, I'll move them around a table or have them climb up different objects in the room. To add dialogue, I can do voiceover work, or I can cut out pieces of paper and add word bubbles.

Selfishly, I do these for my own enjoyment as much as for the kids' education. They are a blast to make. I don't think my own children quite understand my job or why I'm always on the floor in the living room playing with toys, but who says teaching shouldn't also be fun?

Characters

POSSIBLE APPLICATIONS: Teacher to Student

"You aren't even worthy to battle me. Maybe if you practice a little more, you might be able to sit in the same room as me, but for now you'll have to deal with my minion, the evil Zak the Yak!" shouted a man dressed in a dark coat and wearing a pirate's eyepatch. "Good luck with that!" he laughed. Kind of creepy!

This, of course, is the dreaded Dr. Vonn Stock, the vilest villain ever to grace the big screen. He is a dastardly fiend whose sole mission is to make Mr. Stock's life miserable. The kids all know this.

A few boos erupt from the back of the room, along with a few laughs. Just another typical day in my class. Dr. Vonn Stock is one of many characters who show up in my classroom videos throughout the year. He is the main villain in my gamified classroom and, of course, my archenemy. He wears a pirate's eyepatch and constantly reminds students about how evil he is by telling them his evil plots.

It's so cheesy, it's like a block of Velveeta—and the kids love it. They like the opportunity to be kids and laugh at the teacher being silly. They have plenty of opportunities to look at the negative things in the world, so sometimes it's nice just to laugh at something absurd.

These characters appear in a wide range of places in my videos. Sometimes they do the daily announcements. Sometimes they pop up in the middle of an ordinary video for a boring topic as comic relief. Sometimes they make a great addition to a lesson we are rolling with in class. Whatever the reason for their inclusion in my room, it's important to engage the students in something fun. This strategy is similar to stop-motion in that it changes things up just enough to get students to pay attention.

If you are going to try something like this, my main suggestion is this: GO ALL OUT! If you are timid or only do a minor change, the kids will call you out on it. You have to SELL it to the kids that this is a ridiculous, over-the-top batch of awesomeness playing out on the screen in front of them.

How do you go all out? For starters, a costume sets the tone for the whole video. It doesn't have to be an elaborate $100 costume from the costume shop—in fact, cheapness can add to the goofiness. Dollar stores are a great source for props like eyepatches, fake mustaches, goofy sunglasses, and so on. Thrift stores and garage sales are also good spots to find bargains. Amazon also has some great costume items for cheap. Or consider checking out those Halloween stores that pop up in October and then disappear for the rest of the year: they have to clear out of those spaces within a few weeks and want to get rid of their inventory. You can usually get random costumes for cheap. Wigs can be a lot of fun as well. Masks, though, have always been a little iffy for me. Sometimes they are so creepy or weird that they don't really fit with the feel of my class-room. If I do go with a mask, I go with the silliest animal I can find. These costumes also make great props for student skits and videos. It's always a good idea to have a costume tub readily available.

Once you have a costume, you need some props to go with it. The bigger the better. Oversized items add to the fun. What says "rock star" better than an oversize guitar and a disco ball spinning in the background? Props are also an exciting way to emphasize a point. If you are introducing the concept of a plot mountain, for instance, why not record a video of a mountain climber pausing his climb to talk to students? Include things like oxygen tanks (coffee thermoses work great for this), some rope around your shoulder, and a giant fake ice axe flailing around in your hands while you talk. You could even have a tiny mountain sitting next to you (not that I'm speaking from experience here or anything).

My favorite way to use characters is to have a combination of in-class and video characters in the same lesson. In September last year, we were partway through our class novel *Peak*, by Roland Smith. The main character was getting ready to jump on a plane to head to Tibet. I knew the students would be reading about that journey in class, so how could I bring that to life?

"Do you have your ticket?" I asked the first student in line to enter my room that day. He looked at me like I was the usual amount of crazy. "No ticket? Hmm," I said and continued down the line. I was dressed in a suit and tie with a name tag pinned to my jacket.

"Oh, that's right!" I said when I got to the end of the line. "You guys had a set of tickets waiting for you at the front desk." I then passed out a set of paper tickets and let the students enter the room. As soon as they entered, they saw all the desks lined up in two long columns.

After they were all situated, I closed the door and pressed play on the projector. The "captain" made his announcements ("Welcome to Stock Airlines...") then asked the "passengers" to get out their in-flight reading materials (their novels), sit back, relax, and enjoy the flight. The students all looked around the room and followed the instructions. When we "took off," I played a stock video of the sky outside. (You can find plenty of videos like this on YouTube.)

Partway through the hour I walked down the aisle and passed out in-flight snacks. The best thing to do in situations like this is to never break character. At one point, the principal stopped by to ask me a question. I looked shocked and asked him how he was able to fly all the way up here to deliver that message. Another hour, we had to walk down to our new state-of-the-art cafeteria. (In fact, we are the only airline with a complete cafeteria built into our airplane.)

The kids had a blast and spent more time focused on reading than any other day before. Once we arrived at our destination—Nepal—I played another video announcement from the captain. Then the bell rang, and I thanked the students for flying Stock Airlines. For the rest of the day, I could hear students asking students in later class sessions if they had their ticket for their flight or if they had checked out the fancy new in-flight cafeteria.

These experiences get kids excited to come to school and engage in the content. If you can hook them in and then deliver amazing content, you'll have the kids rocking the classroom with that Awesome Sauce.

CHARACTER VIDEO

Ingredients:

recording device (I usually just use my phone)

tripod (optional)

script

costume

props

Awesome Sauce

Prep Time: 5 to 15 minutes

Recording Time: 5 to 15 minutes

Difficulty: ● ● ○ ○ ○

Check out this example: youtu.be/850C9H11VYc

Directions:

1. Choose a setting that fits with the character.

2. Choose a costume that exaggerates the features of the character. It needs to be very clear within a couple of seconds who the character is supposed to be.

3. Include props that fit with the character.

4. Record the video, going through the script. The more over-the-top a character video is, the better.

5. Post the video on YouTube. If you don't want students to see the video ahead of time, post it unlisted.

Here are some of the characters I've brought into the classroom:

- Dr. Vonn Stock
- Superhero
- Secret Agent
- Flight Attendant
- Batman
- Scientist
- Call to Action Man
- Secret Agent Academy Recruiter

TRAVEL *Videos*

POSSIBLE APPLICATIONS:
Teacher to Student

Several years ago, my wife and I flew to Washington, D.C., for an awards ceremony (2016 National School Board Association's "20 to Watch" recipient right here). The trip was amazing. We had a few hours to do a little bit of sightseeing. We saw the Washington Monument, the Holocaust Memorial Museum, and the White House. What a great opportunity—that many of my students may never be able to experience.

Any time I go on a trip like that, I always try to record at least one video. Sometimes it's stock footage for a video I may make in the future. Other times it's specific footage I'm looking for, or the location sparks an idea. In this case, we were in front of the White House, and I decided to record my morning announcements.

This is the power of video, the internet, and Google Classroom. At 8:00 a.m., I recorded my daily announcements. I recorded it in two takes (the first one had someone walk in front of the camera)—about seven minutes total. By 8:15 a.m. I had the announcements posted on Google Classroom and ready for my students. In that short amount of time, I was able to show students a quick glimpse of something they may not have seen before, give them context for some things they might read, and remind them that the places they hear about are real.

My favorite video I recorded was during a ghost hunt, because why **wouldn't** you record a video in a haunted prison at 2:00 a.m.? My wife, some teacher friends, and I all trekked out to Missouri State Penitentiary to investigate "ghost sightings." I'm not a huge believer in that stuff, but a tour of a creepy prison in the middle of the night sounded like an adventure I couldn't pass up.

For hours, we poked around different cells, explored the underground tunnels, and checked out room after room of aging metal, rust-stained bed frames, and peeling paint. The walls echoed, giving an eerie feeling. The more we looked

RECORDING ON LOCATION

Ingredients:

recording device (I usually just use my phone)

tripod (optional, however not as easy to set up in random locations)

awesome location

Awesome Sauce

Prep Time: 2 to 5 minutes

Recording Time: 5 to 20 minutes

Difficulty: ● ● ● ● ●

Directions:

1. Set a goal to record at least one video in any location that might be interesting to students.

2. Go to your location (vacation spot, woods behind your house, strange rock you saw as you were driving home from work one day).

3. Come up with your connections to content. The hardest part is getting in the mindset to look for classroom connections everywhere you go.

4. Consider sound quality. Record a sample video to see what the sound records like.

5. Make adjustments to improve sound, including moving locations slightly. Wherever possible, find wind barriers, such as buildings or trees.

6. Record your video.

7. Save your video in a location you will be able to come back to easily.

Check out this example: youtu.be/2jC4uCRmS6c

the more I realized: THIS MUST BE DR. VONN STOCK'S SECRET LAIR! I needed to get some footage. I had absolutely no idea what I wanted to use it for, but I didn't want to miss the chance.

That is why, at 2:00 a.m., I was running down the halls yelling "They're after me, they're after me!" Then I crouched down inside of one of the cells and whispered "You have to help me!" and "How do I get out of here?!" At one point I found a panel of buttons on the wall. I went up and recorded myself pointing to the buttons and pretending to open a secret door.

I have no idea what everyone else on this ghost hunt thought of my antics, but I didn't care. I was a teacher on a mission, and I was going to get what I needed. That footage made it into a video of Special Agent A from my game asking the students to rescue him. Of course, after all of that work, the students insisted the video *must* have been filmed in my basement. I told them if that's what my basement looks like, they need to be calling the police, not playing along with my game.

ORGANIZING STOCK FOOTAGE

Ingredients:

recorded footage

online storage

Awesome Sauce

Prep Time: 10 to 15 minutes

Recording Time: None

Difficulty: ● ● ● ● ●

Directions:

1. Before uploading your footage from your device, rewatch it and delete anything absolutely unusable (e.g., too blurry to see anything, someone in the background interrupting the shot).

2. Upload your footage to your online storage.

3. Sort the footage into folders.

4. Possible folder labels: Nature, Running, City, Walking, Dungeon, Landmarks.

5. Add a subfolder in each of the above folders titled "Used." There's nothing wrong with reusing footage, but it's helpful to know if you have used it recently.

6. At the end of the year, look through each folder at any footage that hasn't been used. Decide whether you might use it in the future or not.

8

The Kids Menu:
Creating Videos with Students

Students *love* to create! They are used to being consumers of content. These videos will showcase how students can be creators of content and use that creator's mindset to learn new material.

READING *Recordings*

POSSIBLE APPLICATIONS: Students to Community, Students to Students

When I was in middle school, I was required to keep a log of the books I was reading. Each night, I was supposed to write down how many minutes I read, and one of my parents was supposed to sign it. The teacher would check the signature and give me credit for the reading.

I read constantly. I loved to read. I would stay up late trying to sneak in a few pages using the light from the hallway. I would read when I was supposed to be working on assignments for class. I would read at the doctor, at the dentist, or on any errand I went on with my mom.

What I did **not** do was log my reading. I would forget, or the paper would be all the way upstairs and I wouldn't want to go get it, or I would lose the paper.

I rarely had the pages and times written down, so a typical Monday morning would go something like this: On the way to school, I would remember about my form. A panic would start in my stomach. I'd frantically search through my backpack, just in case elves had magically filled out my form for me. No luck. If I found the form, I'd start writing guesstimates of what I read. Maybe a few minutes here, a few minutes there. Oops, it looks too uniform—I should probably change up the amount of time. And I probably would have written in different pens, so I would find a different color pen to fill in parts of the form. Then I would ask my mom to sign it—while she was driving. I'd put the paper in my backpack and turn it in at school. Then the cycle would repeat again the next Monday. All. Year. Long.

I had other friends who would simply make up times they read. Sometimes they would even make up books they read, or they would just cycle through the same couple of books all year. Sometimes they got caught. Other times they didn't.

My point here is that these reading logs for teachers' assessment purposes weren't beneficial to anyone. While it's true that I use reading logs in my class today, their purpose is different. The students log the time they are reading in class. They log what page they start on and compare their reading progress from week to week. They don't get a grade on this—grades are reserved for their written reflections about their reading habits for the week, where I expect honesty. If they say they didn't read that week because they got bored with their book and didn't know what to pick out next, they get credit for that. I just push them on how they are going to improve for next week. The log isn't the learning; it's the goal setting and personal reflection that go with the learning and help students grow as readers.

I use video as part of the students' weekly outside reading log. Every week they are required to record a video about their reading and turn it in on Google Classroom. Sometimes I tell them what to record, and sometimes I give them options, but they are usually one of three types of videos:

1. **Student read-aloud videos.** Students often struggle with reading out loud. It's embarrassing when they don't know the correct word. Middle schoolers feel like their voices are awkward, and you know the boys' voices will hit that mortifying puberty squeak at some point. But I want to hear them reading out loud to me. I want to hear the cadence of their voices, the speed of their reading, and where they are getting stuck.

   This is the most common type of video I assign. Students have to record themselves reading for ten to fifteen minutes—that's it. They just read into the camera. I'm the only one who sees it, so there isn't the pressure of a full class. If certain students read especially well, I'll sometimes ask them if I can share their videos.

   These videos have been a game changer. I learn so much about the students' reading habits from them. If students are already masterful readers, I'll challenge them to try new things like reading characters with different voices or adding emotion to the readings.

   I can also use the videos to request additional interventions. For instance, I had one student who I believed might have a speech impediment. I'm not an expert, but we have a speech pathologist in the building who is. Instead of just describing to the pathologist what I was hearing, I was able to share some of the readings and get this student the support she needed.

   I also use these recordings to track reading growth, as do the students— which leads to the next kind of video.

READING RECORDING VIDEOS

Ingredients:

student recording devices

book

Awesome Sauce

Prep Time: 2 to 5 minutes

Recording Time: 10 to 15 minutes

Level of difficulty: ● ● ● ● ●

Directions:

1. Ask the students to:
   a. Find a quiet location.
   b. Open their book.
   c. Push record.
   d. Read their book for ten to fifteen minutes.
   e. Send you their recordings.
   f. Repeat weekly.

2. It isn't always possible to listen to every student's recording every week, but you can track progress over time by listening to recordings by one quarter of your students one week, another quarter of the students the following week, and so on. That way, once every four weeks you'll be able to listen to one recording by each student.

2. **Student reflection videos.** About once a month, I have students record reflection videos. They rewatch their own videos and explain what they are doing well, then share a reading goal they have. It's incredible to watch. Over the course of the year, many of my students become finely tuned to their own learning abilities. The most important thing is that they are diving into that metacognitive realm. They are thinking about their thinking, taking a deep dive into that gray matter.

3. **Book review.** I have students record videos sharing what they like/dislike about books they finish reading. They follow a simple structure of summarizing the book, sharing three pros/cons of the book and giving the book a letter grade. This kind of video is described further in the next section.

One interesting side benefit of these videos is the peek I get into the lives of my students. I can often hear a lot of noise from little brothers and sisters in the background, or I'll see videos recorded in restaurants where their parents work. It gives me a better understanding of where the students are doing the bulk of their homework. This insight helps me provide students with the specific tools they might need to be successful.

Goal SETTING

I remember the first time I asked my students to set a goal for themselves. I was teaching a reading intervention class called Read 180, and I wanted the students to set a goal for the number of books they would read that semester. I posted the question on the board:

"How many books are you going to read this semester?"

. . . and I waited.

If you have taught for any amount of time, you can probably guess what the responses were like. Students submitted a range of responses, from "books are stuped" (yes, spelled that way) to "10000000000 books." Obviously, these students struggled with goal setting. They had set goals in the past, but they didn't understand the framework or purpose of a goal, and they had never effectively tracked their progress towards a goal.

Reflection is a **huge** part of developing as a student. It's almost impossible for students to take ownership of their learning if they don't know how to set an effective goal and then reflect on it. After looking at this colossal failure, I knew I needed to revise my thinking and go back to the simplest parts when it came to goal setting and reflection with students.

I tried multiple variations. Some worked better than others. Some were epic failures from which I was able to learn. Ultimately, I devised a system to teach kids how to set goals first and then reflect on them.

First, I share with students that I have set goals and failed, and that I have also set goals and succeeded. For example, I set a goal a few years ago (it was actually a New Year's resolution) to work out three nights a week, every week. The plan was great. I was pumped up. I downloaded an app that gave me different workouts I could do from home. I enlisted my wife's support. I was ready.

The first two weeks of the plan I worked out three nights a week. The third week I even added in a fourth day. I was still psyched. Then the app glitched and broke. I couldn't use my app. I'm sure there were other apps I could have downloaded, but I didn't want to go through the work. I gave up. My goal didn't even last the month of January.

I failed for these reasons:

- I wasn't super committed to the plan.

- The plan was hard work, and I didn't care about it enough to persevere if times got tough.

- I didn't set myself up for success. I was doing my workouts at the end of the day, when I was already tired. This made me less likely to want to push through.

- I didn't have an accountability partner.

On the flip side, my wife and I recently went on a weight-loss journey. We set a goal to lose weight. My ultimate goal was to lose fifty pounds. I've tried weight-loss goals before, so I was worried that this one might fail, too. We dove in and from April through July, we lost more than forty pounds each.

We succeeded for these reasons:

- We worked together. We constantly checked in with each other and kept each other on track.

- We came up with recipes we could share, kept bad food out of the house, and banded together when we went to family gatherings full of delicious treats.

- We found a plan that we could stick with. We used Weight Watchers and followed guidelines for success.

I share both of these examples and explanations with students, and then we talk about times when they have set goals. Most of them can point to a time in school when they tried to set a goal. We talk about why it succeeded or didn't succeed. Then we start setting their goals.

I usually have students set a goal with a couple of things in mind: it needs to be measurable, it needs to have a time limit, and it needs to be realistic. If I had students set a goal at this point, many of the kids would have no idea how to make sure they're realistic. We need some sort of baseline criteria. For reading goals, I have students read for ten minutes and measure how many pages they read (the page number they ended on minus the page number they started on). Then we multiply that by six, and they have their pages-per-hour score. Then we talk about how much they should be reading each week. My goal for them is about twenty minutes a day, so I tell them to figure out how many pages they

GOAL VIDEOS

Ingredients:

recording device

tripod (optional)

goal

Awesome Sauce

Prep Time: 5 to 7 minutes

Recording Time: 3 to 7 minutes

Difficulty: ● ● ● ● ●

Directions:

1. Students will think about a weekly goal they have. Depending on your purposes, these could be academic, personal, social, and so on.

2. Students record their videos and answer the following questions:

   a. What is your goal this week?

   b. What roadblocks do you see coming up?

   c. How will you overcome those roadblocks?

3. Students share the videos with their accountability group.

4. Repeat every week.

should read each week if they read for two hours a week. They freak out a little bit when I tell them we are doing math in a language arts goal-setting lesson, but it's important that they see how the numbers add up.

Once students have their weekly pages goal, they record a goal video. The videos are extremely simple. Students have to answer three questions:

1. What is your goal this week?

2. What roadblocks do you see coming up? (e.g., soccer practice, big social studies project due.)

3. How will you overcome those roadblocks?

That's it. They answer those three questions and post the video on Google Classroom. I can watch the videos and comment on them, but the videos aren't about me. They're about the students verbalizing a commitment to meet those goals. The goals don't matter without follow-up, so each week we discuss students' progress toward meeting them. About once a month they record reflection videos where they walk through their successes and struggles.

Accountability groups help, too. Students meet in groups to discuss their progress toward their goals. They encourage each other and help come up with solutions to overcome obstacles. Sometimes that little piece of having to tell someone how you did is enough motivation to stay on track. Do kids lie sometimes? Of course, but not nearly as much as you would think. Most kids like being in control of their own goals.

This doesn't apply solely to language arts, either. I use the same video strategies in homeroom. Students set a wide range of goals. Sometimes they set kindness goals, where they try to say one nice thing to someone in each class or sit next to someone new in the cafeteria. Sometimes they set organization goals, such as to fill out their planners each hour or to put all of their papers in the correct folders. (Who knew the bottom of your backpack wasn't the place for loose papers?) Once you get to a point where students can set their own goals independent of you, you've met your target.

NEWS *Broadcasts*

My first year teaching, I took over the school newspaper. When I graduated from college, I was three credits shy of a minor in journalism, but I still didn't feel prepared to teach a class about putting together the school newspaper, and I sure didn't know how to navigate a digital age newspaper class. Not only did we put together the print news, but we also needed to tackle blogging, podcasting, and video news broadcasting.

I felt overwhelmed, but as usual I dove in headfirst. The first year I focused on mastering print news, interview etiquette, writing strategies, and so on. But once I felt like I had my footing, I rolled out podcasts and blogs. Soon we added a video news broadcast.

It wasn't great.

We didn't have the tools we needed to do this easily. Only a few kids had cell phones, and we weren't at 1:1 iPads yet, so we relied on a flip camera. The image quality was grainy and the sound was difficult to hear, but the kids had so much fun. As the years went on, we honed the news broadcast, and now the kids have the skills needed every time we go to record it.

I've taught this class off and on for a few years now. I miss the class when I don't teach it, and I wanted to bring the thrill of creating a video production to my other classes, so I decided to bring news broadcasts into language arts (and they can be applied to just about any other class, too).

NEWS BROADCAST

Ingredients:

recording device

tripod (optional)

script

costumes

products for commercials (optional)

Awesome Sauce

Prep Time: 60 to 90 minutes

Recording Time: 75 to 120 minutes

Difficulty: ● ● ● ● ●

Directions:

1. Students read a text (news article, textbook, novel, etc.) and select the three to five events that are most important for the news broadcast.
2. Divide the students up into news teams of three to four students.
3. In groups of three, students select from the following roles:
   a. The Director/Camera Operator, in charge of keeping the production on schedule, choosing locations for recording, and operating the camera
   b. Reporters 1 and 2, in charge of writing scripts and reading them on camera

* In groups of four, divide up the director and camera operator roles.

4. Students compare their lists, choose the three to five most important events, then work together to find facts and evidence to fully explain the events.
5. Students then work in individual roles:
   a. Director/Camera Operator scouts out locations, gets props, and plans out a recording schedule using a storyboard.
   b. Reporter 1 writes scripts for two stories.
   c. Reporter 2 writes scripts for two stories.
6. Groups record all their videos.
7. A high-tech version would be to use advanced video-editing software like iMovie to edit the video together. A low-tech version would be to use a slideshow program and include a video on each slide.
8. Host a premiere of the final videos and celebrate everyone's Awesome Sauce.

Alternative:

1. Instead of having small groups of three to four students forming news teams, have larger groups of six to ten students.
2. The roles in this case would be as follows:
   a. Director, in charge of keeping the production on schedule (extremely important in this format)
   b. Camera Operators 1 and 2, who choose locations for recording and operating the camera. These two are also in charge of assisting the director.
   c. Reporters 1 and 2, in charge of writing scripts and reading them on camera
   d. Anchors 1 and 2, in charge of introducing the reporters and their scripts, both of which they write
   e. More reporters as needed

My favorite iteration of this strategy was during a unit on the Montgomery Bus Boycott. The students were reading the book *Freedom Walkers* by Russell Friedman. I grouped them into news teams and challenged them to put together a news broadcast about the events from the book.

In their groups they had to define their roles, manage their time, and wisely choose the information they used. I gave them a week to select the content they felt was most important for their videos. This was insightful. I always think I'm clear in highlighting important moments from the book, but it was interesting to see what the students pulled out. The broadcast also gave me a clear understanding of what students understood or didn't understand. It not only gave me valuable information on what needed to be retaught, but it also gave me clarity for the following year on things that needed to be addressed throughout the reading process. For example, the first two chapters of the book actually take place a few years before the boycott and provide background information leading up to the actual boycott. After watching the videos I realized that students didn't make the connection that these events took place at an earlier time period.

Once students finished with their news broadcasts, we had a quick reflection and talk about why they made the choices they did and what suggestions they had for my students for next year. We also talked through the process, their role in the recording, their strengths and struggles. They reflected on who they were as group members and how they could be an even more productive group next time.

Some kids even exceeded expectations and added commercials for products available during the time period we were studying. The project offered creativity and opportunities for a practical application of their learning.

In the future I would love to celebrate their accomplishments with a movie premiere. If possible, I would like to get the auditorium and have a big screening complete with popcorn. We could showcase the students' news broadcasts and enjoy the hard work they put into them.

STUDENT *Recordings* FOR EDITING

Students aren't naturally great editors. At the beginning of the year, when they first sit down to edit their classmates' papers, I know they will fall into one of two categories.

Students in the first group don't know what to do when they edit. They sit down to a piece of writing and "read" through it. I can always spot these kids from across the room. They look intently at the page and make a big show of reading the page. They may even flip it over a few times to indicate they are obviously taking this seriously and reading it multiple times. Then they take out their pen and write "good job!" or ":-)," or find some minor punctuation error and fix it. Sometimes they invent a punctuation error just to have something to write down. Then they pass the page back.

Students in the second group skim through the writing and finish their "reading" before I'm even done explaining the instructions. Then they look at me and say "Mr. Stock, it was perfect. There wasn't anything to change in it."

Neither one of these groups is helpful. The editing doesn't improve the writing and often leaves both the editor and the writer frustrated.

To counteract this, I give the students structure. They go through the same steps when they edit or revise their own writing as they do when editing a peer's paper. The first step is for them to read through the writing and record it. This is awkward the first few times they do it, but it turns into a powerful tool. Students catch on quickly to trouble areas when they stumble over a section of writing.

After they have recorded themselves reading the paper out loud, students comment on three things:

1. One to two things the writer did well

2. One to two areas for improvement

3. One final thought

That's it. I keep it simple. Sometimes I want them to edit all the punctuation or grammar mistakes, but most of the time they don't pay attention to those notes. It's not worth the time it takes for most assignments. and I would rather invest that time in making these recordings.

VIDEO PEER EDITING

Ingredients:

recording device (I usually just use my phone)

three copies of the writing piece to be edited

two highlighters of different colors

Awesome Sauce

Prep Time: 15 to 20 minutes

Recording Time: 10 to 15 minutes

Difficulty: ● ● ● ● ●

Directions:

1. Have the students partner up and swap papers.

2. Video 1: Students record themselves reading through the paper out loud. They should highlight positives with one color and room for reflection with the other.

3. Video 2: Students record a reflection answering the following three questions:

   a. What are one or two things the writer did well?

   b. What are one or two areas for improvement?

   c. What is one final thought you have?

4. After students have practiced this strategy a few times, they can combine the two videos into one.

5. Students return the paper to their partners and share the two reflection videos. They can either swap devices to watch it, e-mail it to the other person, or AirDrop it if using an Apple device.

6. Repeat the process with another set of partners.

Once students have finished a video, they record another one for a different student. I usually have them try to do at least three recordings during class. Then they can watch the recordings other students did for them to get the feedback on their own writing.

If you want to kick it up a notch, you could also have parents record feedback on their children's writing. I know a lot of parents who would love to help their children but don't know where to start. This assignment gives parents some direction on how to help out.

Public Service ANNOUNCEMENTS

This is one of those anchor projects that sticks with you from year to year. I started doing it about five years ago and have done it in some form almost every year since then.

Few things frustrate students more than learning something that doesn't seem to have a connection to real life, so I try to find as many relevant real-world writing assignments as possible, and I love this one. We spend the first few weeks of school (once we start diving into content) reading about exotic animals. The kids enjoy reading articles about pythons that attack their owners, people who try to form their own zoos in their backyards (both legally and illegally), and "the lion whisperer."

I used to guide students through a persuasive essay after they finished reading all of these texts, and it was boring. Then I discovered the art of the public service announcement (PSA). PSAs are those ad campaigns intended to persuade you to feel a certain way about a topic. To show the students what a PSA is, I direct them to examples on the Ad Council's website, adcouncil.org, which has numerous resources and examples of PSAs. We usually talk about the PSAs for recycling, because that's a subject all the students are already familiar with.

After we've figured out what a PSA is, I give students their challenge. They have to record their own PSA answering the following question: "Should exotic animals be owned as pets?" They then spend the next week working with their "film crew," coming up with their own public service announcement campaign to convince people that owning an exotic animal as a pet is a good or bad idea.

The results turn out fantastic. Most kids are passionate about animals. They enjoy adding sad music in the background and showing pictures of poor, defenseless animals locked in cages. Or they'll use pictures of kids and say something like "Would you trust a lion around *your* kids?" If we have time, I'll also work in a discussion of effective persuasive techniques.

I require students to have evidence to support their claims, which is always a challenge for them. They often don't know what to say and don't have the facts to back up what they are saying. When they show me something, I ask them how they know it's true. This throws them off, but I want them to realize that if they want to state something as fact, they need to be able to back it up with evidence.

Finally, we showcase the PSAs. Students write scripts, which I grade. They also fill out an evaluation discussing how their film crews worked together. It always surprises me how honest the kids are. They will tell you flat out if they feel that someone in their group isn't pulling their own weight. It's also a good moment when they can watch the other students' videos and see how theirs line up with their classmates'.

PUBLIC SERVICE ANNOUNCEMENTS

Ingredients:

recording device

tripod (optional)

scripts

Awesome Sauce

Prep Time: 60 to 90 minutes
(a lot of time is spent on
research for the script)

Recording Time: 30 to
45 minutes

Difficulty: ● ● ● ● ●

Directions:

1. Before starting this project, students should have extensive knowledge of the topic, whether it's from reading texts, watching videos, exploring websites, or some combination of those.

2. Have students make a T-chart of both sides of the topic. Some topics may be easy to come up with multiple sides for, while others might be a little more challenging. In the case of recycling, for example, one reason to argue against it could be that the factories that recycle materials create air pollution that is also bad for the environment.

3. Have the students brainstorm at least three reasons on each side of the debate. This will be important later, even if students know which side they are on.

4. Have the students circle the side of the T-chart they feel the strongest about.

5. Have students go to one side of the room or the other, depending on which side they are on.

6. Have the students break into groups of four and divide into these roles:

   a. Director/Camera Operator, in charge of keeping the video on track

   b. On-Screen 1 and 2, who help with the script and on camera talent

7. Groups choose the *best* three reasons from all of their lists.

8. Groups look for evidence to support their reasons.

9. A good argument gives a nod to the opposition, so have groups look at the other column and come up with one reason from the other side that they can prove is wrong. Then find evidence that supports why that reason is wrong.

10. Divide work by roles:

    a. On-Screen 1 and 2 work on writing a fluid script for all of this evidence.

    b. Director/Camera Operator work on visuals for the video and scout out a location to record.

11. Practice recording the PSA.

12. Record the PSA.

13. Have a central location to post all of these PSAs so that others can watch them. It's especially helpful if you can share the PSAs with a community organization.

Rules FOR NEXT YEAR

Kids don't value my opinion. Wait, let me revise that: when it comes to how to survive my class, kids don't value my opinion as much as those of their peers. My class is weird. I know it. My kids learn it on Day One, and most kids hear rumors about it before they ever walk into my room. They need advice on the ins and outs of surviving the chaos that is Room 508.

At the end of the year, my students know all the tips and tricks for dealing with me. I can be quirky, and I definitely have my pet peeves like most people. For example, I hate being asked a question that I just explained because you were busy working on something else instead of listening to me.

To wrap up the year, I give students the challenge of creating a Top Ten List of rules for surviving my class. These videos are always fun and often eye-opening. Sometimes I don't realize I'm doing something until the students point it out. Other times the videos just make me laugh, because I know I'm weird.

It's a great way to wrap up the year. On the last few days of school we watch the videos and reminisce.

"RULES FOR SURVIVING MY CLASS" VIDEOS

Ingredients:

recording device

tripod (optional)

rules script

Awesome Sauce

Prep Time: 30 to 45 minutes

Recording Time: 15 to 30 minutes

Difficulty: ● ● ● ● ●

Directions:

1. Each student should write down five to ten rules for surviving your class.

2. Break the students into groups of three to four.

3. Have the students in each group divide into these roles:

   a. Director/Camera Operator, in charge of keeping the video on track

   b. On-Screen 1 and 2, in charge of helping with the script and on camera talent

4. Groups combine their lists together and write scripts of ten rules to survive your class.

5. Directors/Camera Operators scope out locations for the shoot while the on-screen members revise the script.

6. Groups record their videos.

7. If there is time, students can add sound effects and music in the background using either a high-tech method like GarageBand and iMovie or a low-tech version like playing the sound effects on another device next to the camera at the appropriate time.

8. Have groups share their videos with you either through e-mail or by posting to YouTube.

9. Have a movie premiere where the class watches everything new students need to know to survive your class.

10. Save the videos to share with new students the following year.

9

Video Tips

TOP 10

1. Limit your retakes.

2. Use plenty of guests.

3. Create a YouTube channel to house all your videos.

4. Create playlists on YouTube for different purposes.

5. Purchase a decent tripod (around $50).

6. Be aware of where you are looking when you are recording. If you use a script, tape it as close to the camera as possible.

7. Record in a location with the best sound options.

8. Invite students to help record videos.

9. Record everywhere.

10. Do it.

TOP 10 *Expanded*

1. Limit your retakes.

Five years ago, I didn't have a YouTube channel. I didn't record videos or post them online. I didn't do *anything* with video. Why?

I was afraid.

I was afraid that I would stutter, or that I would say "um" through the whole thing. I was afraid that students wouldn't like it or that I would look stupid. Fear kept me from creating epic content for my students.

Then something changed. I decided to just try recording videos. I recorded my first video, and it wasn't great. I was afraid to share it with my students, so I rerecorded it twenty times. Finally, I thought I had a perfect video I could share with them. I was wrong. I still made mistakes. But an interesting thing happened: the kids loved it. They didn't care that I messed up. In fact, they loved seeing that I make just as many errors as they do. After that, I refused to rerecord a video more than three times, and I stick to that rule to this day.

If you spend your time worrying about what will go wrong, you miss out on all the ways things could go right. You miss out on all the awesome opportunities your videos could open up for your students. Don't be afraid. Embrace the imperfections. Enjoy it!

2. Use plenty of guests.

Most students have that one adult in the building they connect with, the one who listens to them and knows them best. It may be you, or it may be the secretary in the front office, or it may be the art teacher. The important thing is to try to include as many of these people in your videos as possible. Getting other adults involved in your videos gives you the best chance to engage students. It also makes your life easier. And your guests don't always have to be "real" people from your school—Batman may have shown up in my videos once or twice.

3. Create a YouTube channel to house all your videos.

You need a hub for all these amazing videos you are creating, a one-stop shop for anything that might benefit your students. You'll be shocked at the number of students who come into your class for the first time and can already tell you a lot about your class and upcoming lessons. They will stalk you. They will look through every video you've posted.

It. Is. Awesome.

YouTube is also a great way to stay connected to students and parents. Share your YouTube channel link with parents and encourage them to subscribe. If they do, they will automatically get notified when you post something new. This will always keep them up to date with the most recent happenings in your class.

YOUTUBE PRIVACY SETTINGS

YouTube currently has three settings for posting videos:

1. **PUBLIC.** This is usually the default setting. It allows you to post videos for anyone to see. These videos are searchable.

2. **UNLISTED.** These are videos that can only be viewed by clicking on the video link directly. These aren't searchable and are generally secure. The only concern is that the person you share the link with could also share the link with someone else without your knowledge.

3. **PRIVATE.** These videos can only be viewed by inviting the user to view the video through an e-mail invite. This is the most secure setting, but at the moment only fifty people can be invited to view a video at one time.

4. Create YouTube playlists for different purposes.

If you're like me, you overload your channel with videos. If you post too many different videos, students and parents won't know which ones they should watch. So, put the most important ones in playlists, which help you to keep them organized by type.

I create videos for teachers, parents, and students. Students don't care about the latest features in the gradebook program, just like teachers don't care that Dr. Vonn Stock is using similes and metaphors to attack a pirate ship.

5. Purchase a decent tripod (around $50) and use it.

I have a hard time following this piece of advice. If you look at a lot of my videos, especially my daily announcements, you'll notice that a lot of them are shaky. I usually forget to set up my tripod, and that's the result. For a quick announcement video I'm not too concerned, but for more important videos I like to make sure to set up a tripod. It gives the video a more polished feel and makes it easier for students to watch.

Most tripods come with various attachments to let you switch between different devices. I have one for my phone and one for my iPad. The tripod I'm currently using (my second one) was about $50 on Amazon. My first one broke. Apparently if you fall down some stairs with it, the tripod might break. (Thankfully there was nobody there to see it happen.)

6. Be aware of where you are looking when you are recording. If you use a script, tape it as close to the camera as possible.

Be aware of where the camera is located on your recording device. Look directly into the camera. If you spend an entire video looking down at a script it will be obvious, and your videos will lose that professional flair. I can't tell you how many videos my newspaper classes recorded with the students looking down at their page and never once looking up. Your audience wants to see your eyes. It should feel like you are talking directly to them.

One way to help with this is to tape your script as close to the camera as possible. That way if you have to look at it from time to time, it isn't obvious. It looks more natural. I'd also recommend writing a bulleted list instead of a word-for-word script. You can start with a script, but eventually whittle it down to a few points. This helps the dialogue to flow more naturally and keeps you from sounding like a robot. (Unless you are recording a robot video, in which case, carry on.)

7. Record in a location with the best sound options.

The difference between a good video and a great one is often determined by sound quality, which can go wrong in so many ways. The first thing to think about is your location and background noise. If you are recording with the built-in microphone on your recording device, record in a quiet room. Even with a good microphone, you should pay attention to the background noise. If you're not careful, you'll have a disruptive background noise after you're done recording, and you can't do much about it after that. Avoid recording outside if at all possible: wind is recording's worst nightmare, and even if there is very little wind, recording without getting a whooshing noise is extremely difficult.

8. Invite students to help record videos.

Students are the most creative people in the school, especially if you make it a place where they can safely take risks. They are fearless and come up with amazing ideas for videos. I love to bring students into any video I can. Every once in a while, a random student will appear in one of my announcement videos. Chances are that student happened to come into my room during my planning period to ask me a question or drop off something from the office. If I'm recording, I'll make that student a part of my video.

On one occasion, I had a student who wasn't interested in my class at all. He wasn't a fan of reading and didn't want to participate in the lessons. He was constantly trying to goof off or make noises to get others off track. One day after school, I was getting ready to record a video when I saw him wandering around in the halls. I pulled him into my room and asked if he would be my cameraman for the day. I didn't really need one—a tripod would have done just as well—but I knew this would be a great opportunity to connect. At the end of the video, I added a clip of him and a shout-out to my rock star cameraman. The next day, when I showed the video to the class, he was stoked. He had so much pride in that video and wanted to show it off to everyone. After that, he wanted to help out more and started looking for ways to contribute in class. He became an active member of the classroom instead of a passive bystander. Rainbows and sunshine didn't instantly fall from the heavens—he still didn't like reading—but it was definitely a step in the right direction.

9. Record everywhere.

A haunted prison, the White House, Diagon Alley at Universal Studios: I have recorded videos for my students in all of these places. I constantly record videos anytime I go anywhere. Vacations, work trips, ghost hunts—any new place is a great opportunity. Most of the time it just takes five minutes to shoot a quick video. Sometimes I record random stock footage I may want to include in a future video. Other times I record a quick history lesson. The new locations provide a nice change of pace for the students.

These videos can add relevance to class by showcasing real places students are learning about or giving real context to content. Language arts teachers can share videos of places where novels take place. Social studies teachers can record at famous battlefields or historical landmarks. Science teachers can take videos where famous inventions were created. Students get a visual cue for content they may only see pictures of or read about. Sometimes what students read is disconnected from the real world, and this strategy brings the two together.

10. Do it.

The biggest thing holding most people back is fear. Fear that the video won't be perfect. Fear that you won't know how to record a video. Fear that your ideas are dumb. Fear that the students won't connect with the videos. And you know what? You're right. All of those things could happen. But guess what happens if they do?

Life. Goes. On. On those rare occasions when a video doesn't quite work out, you move on.

BUT...

For every video that doesn't work out, there are twenty more that get the kids fired up for learning and engage them in new and exciting ways. That makes it worth it. The value added to the classroom has so much more impact than a video that messes up. Failure is just a learning opportunity.

So, dive in and bring the Awesome Sauce to your classroom!

TECHNOLOGY *101*

Just about any video in this book can be completed with the most basic setup. However, as you create more videos, you may want to expand the tools you use to record. Here are some things to consider:

1. **You need a solid surface to record on.** It is almost impossible to hold a camera still while you record. As I said in the Top 10 list, it's best if you

have a tripod, but if you don't, at least find a solid surface to set the camera on. I almost always find some way to set the camera down when I'm filming. It could be as simple as a table or shelf. When I record my announcement videos, I prop up my phone on the handles of a cabinet in my room because it happens to be the perfect height. Over the years I've accumulated more tools. You may want the following:

- a tripod that will hold your device on a table for videos where you want to sit and record talking directly to the camera

- a tripod that will hold your device at a height of 50" to 70" for videos where you want to move in the shot or for standing videos

- a selfie stick for adding unique angles in your videos

2. **You need some way to hit record.** Since you won't be holding the camera, you need a way to push record on your device. For some videos, I don't mind if the viewer sees me lean forward and push record. But if I want a video to look more professional, I have a clicker to push record or I edit out the first few seconds of the video. Most tripods come with a clicker that connects to your device through Bluetooth.

3. **You need some way to capture the sound.** Audio can make the difference between an effective video and one that distracts from the learning. The built-in audio on most devices works just fine when you are starting out, but eventually you may also want the following:

- a condenser microphone that connects to your device

- a lavalier microphone (one that clips to your clothing) that connects to your device

Whichever microphone you go with, make sure it connects to your device. For example, when Apple stopped including a headphone jack on the iPhone, I had to get an adapter for my lavalier microphone.

4. **You need to create the best lighting.** Lighting can be tricky, especially in a school setting. Fluorescent lighting can be dull. You need to make sure there aren't any bright glares on the camera screen. I've been able to get by just fine by recording during the day when possible and making sure to adjust the blinds to allow as much natural light in as I can. When

I don't have natural light, I use a lot of lamps to get the lighting just right. However, you might eventually want to invest in a photography lighting kit.

5. **You need some way to edit your more elaborate videos.** You may want to go all out and edit together an Awesome Sauce video. To do that, you'll need some way to edit the video together. Many devices have built-in editing software. For example, Apple products come with iMovie. Eventually you might want to invest in video-editing software.

6. **You may want to screencast (record your screen).** To screencast, you will need a couple of things: a camera to record video, a microphone to record audio, and an app, website, or software to record the screen. Eventually you may also want a web camera to record the screen (most video-editing software includes a screencasting option).

When I first started recording videos for the classroom, I used my phone and iMovie. That's it! I didn't have any fancy equipment, and the videos turned out great. Each year I add one or two pieces to my collection through grants, gifts from my family, and conferences. Start small and do what you can with what you've got. It's not what you're recording with that matters. It's the Awesome Sauce you add to each video that truly makes a difference.

 To get started check out the Awesome Sauce 101 playlist on YouTube: youtube.com/playlist?list=PLifJz8mRJxI3dCFS0jOCbR0e3JE2US094

CHAPTER 10

What's Next?

Dear Educator,

After reading this book, you have probably figured out that I don't have an elaborate recording studio, and I don't spend hours each day recording videos. Most of the time I record what I can in the moment, with the materials I have on hand.

I have created all of these videos throughout my teaching career (with the exception of the PE examples, for which I consulted some PE teachers and used my experiences with energy break videos). However, each class is different. Some years, the guest videos have a huge impact on student learning, and I devote a lot of time to them. Other years, I have higher numbers of students who need interventions, so I may devote time to recording assignment clarifications and accommodations. The point is that I've never recorded every video in this book in one year, and neither should you. The goal is to provide a resource that you can pull from as needs arise. Each video is another recipe in your teaching recipe box, waiting to be called upon at a moment's notice.

The beauty of videos, especially if you post them on YouTube, is that some of your more evergreen content will be usable for years to come. One of my oldest videos, the video on internal and external conflict from The Brain section of this book, is over six years old but still a valuable tool for introducing the concepts. The kids enjoy the fact that I hadn't grown my beard yet and my daughter was still in kindergarten. Just keep track of what videos you create and organize them in playlists. After a year or two, you will have a channel of content you can use year after year. Reuse the videos that were helpful and move on from the videos that aren't. Over time you'll accumulate a wealth of video content to use throughout your teaching.

We're all in this together. Subscribe to my classroom channel on YouTube and feel free to use any of my videos in your classroom. I'd also love to highlight and share some of the Awesome Sauce you're creating. Share your videos on Twitter with the hashtag #AwesomeSauceEDU.

Soon you'll be creating the Awesome Sauce in your own classroom!

Final thoughts…

 youtu.be/Du25mLPayyQ

Behind the scenes of the final thoughts video…

 youtu.be/pCXuK89wHEo

FOLLOW THE *Author*

For more information, check out my website: mrstockrocks.com

Twitter: @teachlikeaninja

Instagram: @teachlikeaninja

Facebook page: facebook.com/teachlikeaninja

YouTube channel for educators: youtube.com/c/JoshStockisAwesome

YouTube channel for my actual classroom: youtube.com/c/JoshStockRocks

Share the Awesome Sauce with others using the hashtag: #AwesomeSauceEDU

References

Ad Council. (n.d.). adcouncil.org.

Brame, C.J. (2015). Effective educational videos. cft.vanderbilt.edu
/guides-sub-pages/effective-educational-videos

Driscoll, M. P. (2005). Psychology of learning for instruction. Pearson Allyn
and Bacon.

Gonzalez, J. (2014, March 24). Modifying the flipped classroom: The "in-class"
version. edutopia.org/blog/flipped-classroom-in-class-version-jennifer
-gonzalez

Guo, P. J., Kim, J., & Rubin, R. (2014, March 4). How video production affects
student engagement: An empirical study of MOOC videos. citeseerx.ist.psu
.edu/viewdoc/summary?doi=10.1.1.644.4382

Hattie, J. (2010). *Visible learning: a synthesis of over 800 meta-analyses relating to
achievement*. Routledge.

Herculano-Houzel, S. (2009, November 9). The human brain in numbers: a
linearly scaled-up primate brain. ncbi.nlm.nih.gov/pmc/articles
/PMC2776484

Klein, A. (2019, October 29). Teens' online video viewing soared over the past
four years, report finds. blogs.edweek.org/edweek/DigitalEducation/2019/10
/common-sense-online-video-viewing-media.html

Mayer, R. E. (2008, November). Applying the science of learning: evidence-
based principles for the design of multimedia instruction. ncbi.nlm.nih.gov
/pubmed/19014238

Noonoo, S. (2018, December 27). Why flipped learning is still going strong
10 years later. *EdSurge News*. edsurge.com/news/2017-10-03-why-flipped
-learning-is-still-going-strong-10-years-later

Paas, F., Gog, T. V., & Sweller, J. (2010). Cognitive load theory: New conceptualizations, specifications, and integrated research perspectives. *Educational Psychology Review, 22*(2), 115–121. doi.org/10.1007/s10648 -010-9133-8

Rideout, V., & Robb, M. B. (2019, October 28). The Common Sense Census: Media use by tweens and teens, 2019. *Common Sense Media.* commonsensemedia.org/research/the-common-sense-census-media-use-by -tweens-and-teens-2019

Thomson, A., Bridgstock, R., & Willems, C. (2014). "Teachers flipping out" beyond the online lecture: Maximising the educational potential of video. jld.edu.au/article/view/209.html

Index

P

parents

    class trailers and, 15

    involvement in making videos, 25, 84

    opportunities for feedback from, 98

    parents of new students, 21–22

    recap videos and, 26–28

    technology walkthrough videos and, 74–76

    video introductions and, 21–22

    video updates to, 28–30

Paulson, Gary, 34

Peak, 34, 82

pep talks, 24–26

physical education, 66–68

positive affirmation, 13, 24–26, 30–32, 93, 107

PowerPoint, 59, 63

    embedding video in slides, 14

privacy, YouTube privacy settings, 105

public service announcements, 98–100

Q

QR codes

    use with book talk videos, 41

    use with exercise instruction videos, 67–68

    use with guided reading videos, 61

    use with scavenger hunt videos, 44

    use with station instruction videos, 39–40

    use with substitute welcome videos, 74

    use with test accommodation videos, 64–65

    use with video introductions, 22

    use with welcome videos, 18

R

reading

    book talks, 40–41

    guided reading, 60–64

    student-created reading videos, 40, 88–90

recap videos, 26–28

recording videos, best practices for, 104–108, 108–110

retakes, limiting retakes, 104

room tours, 17–18

routines, 12

Rowland, Amber, 3

Rubin, Rob, 5, 8

Rudolph the Red-Nosed Reindeer (Rankin/Bass), 78

S

scavenger hunts, 43–45

school tours, 19–20

screencasting, 110

    student screencasts, 50, 75

    uses for, 36–38, 45–47, 52–54, 74–76

sensory memory, 6, 7

Smith, Roland, 34, 82

Socratic Circles, 34

    modified Socratic Circles, 42–43

sound

    avoiding distracting background noise, 106–107

    See also music

Y

YouTube

  author YouTube channels, 113

  Awesome Sauce 101 playlist on, 4

  embedding video in slides, 14

  having a YouTube channel, 105

  privacy settings, 105

  recap videos and, 27

  use of playlists, 48, 51, 61, 105

  YouTube Audio Library, 16, 26

YouTubers, value of asking students
    about, 4

BOOK IT

FORWARD

AND BE

Awesome!

YOUR OPINION MATTERS

TELL US HOW WE'RE DOING!

Your feedback helps ISTE create the best possible resources for teaching and learning in the digital age. Share your thoughts with the community or tell us how we're doing!

You can:

- Write a review at amazon.com or barnesandnoble.com.

- Mention this book on social media and follow ISTE on Twitter @iste, Facebook @ISTEconnects or Instagram @isteconnects

- Email us at books@iste.org with your questions or comments.